5-10-11

Max—

Enjoy the book. You are a great mentor!

Bob Barry

Bob Bush

Michael Dorn

VOICE of BEDLAM

The Life of Bob Barry

BY
MICHAEL DEAN & BOB BURKE

OKLAHOMA **TRACKMAKER** SERIES

SERIES EDITOR: GINI MOORE CAMPBELL

ASSOCIATE EDITOR: ERIC DABNEY

Publication made possible through the generosity of the following:

Mr. & Mrs. Calvin Anthony
Mr. & Mrs. Clayton I. Bennett
Bob Burke
Jackie Cooper Family
Mr. & Mrs. Lee Allan Smith
Sooner Sports Properties and Learfield Communications
Barry Switzer
University of Oklahoma Intercollegiate Athletics

OKLAHOMA TRACKMAKER SERIES

OKLAHOMA HERITAGE ASSOCIATION

CONTENTS

ACKNOWLEDGMENTS

The story of Bob Barry's life is inextricably intertwined with the athletic traditions of the University of Oklahoma and Oklahoma State University. For a half century, "Big Bob" Barry has vividly described the fortunes of the storied programs for thousands of fans listening by radio.

Many people helped make this project successful. Bob's sons, Frank and Bobby; Bob's co-workers, including television personalities and radio broadcast team partners; and many friends and former coaches were generous in recalling their recollections of his life.

At OSU, we are grateful to Athletic Director Mike Holder and his staff, Director of Media Relations Kevin Klintworth, and football coach Mike Gundy. At OU, President David L. Boren, Athletic Director Joe Castiglione, Associate Athletic Director for Communications Kenny Mossman, Press Secretary Jay Doyle, Lisa Hall, and coaches Bob Stoops and Jeff Capel assisted the project.

Former football and basketball coaches, including Pat Jones, Kelvin Sampson, Billy Tubbs, Leonard Hamilton, Barry Switzer, Merv Johnson, and John MacLeod granted interviews, as did friends of Bob such as Lee Allan Smith, Lee Thompson, Jr., and Don Symcox, who have known Bob longer than have OU and OSU football and basketball fans.

We thank Linda Lynn, Melissa Hayer, Mary Phillips, Robin Davison, and Billie Harry at the Oklahoma Publishing Company for photographic assistance. Our editors, Gini Moore Campbell and Eric Dabney, encouraged us as we waded through a half century of accounts of football and basketball games. A special thank you to Kris Vculek for her excellent design of the book.

As co-authors, this was a labor of love for us. We began our broadcasting careers together in high school and rekindled old times at breakfast meetings at the Classen Grill. Most of all, we thank Bob for opening his life to our questions. At breakfast meetings at the Cracker Barrel, in Bob's home office or living room, where he spends a lot of time watching sporting events on a giant television, he was completely honest about both the high and low points of his life. There will never be another Bob Barry.

—THE AUTHORS

FOREWORD

By David L. Boren, *President, University of Oklahoma*

No one wears the title "Voice of Bedlam" better than Bob Barry. For 49 football seasons, he has been the play-by-play announcer for the annual football game between the University of Oklahoma and Oklahoma State University. For 31 of those seasons, Bob has been the voice of the Sooners and from 1973 to 1990 he was the voice of the Cowboys. In that nearly half century he has called every game of four Heisman Trophy winners—Steve Owens, Jason White, and Sam Bradford at OU, and Barry Sanders at OSU—a feat never duplicated by any other radio sportscaster in history.

Bob has been extremely loyal to OU and its athletic program. In bad times and good times, he has been the voice of optimism and enthusiasm. He began broadcasting OU football games when Bud Wilkinson was head coach and is a link to the storied past of Sooner football. To many fans, Bob is a reassuring voice, giving fans a good feeling that OU always has a chance to win the game. Even in disappointing seasons, Bob champions the coaches and players and looks for something good in every situation.

Bob in many ways represents the best of our Sooner spirit.

CHAPTER ONE

A Close Call

The manner in which I spent my time recovering from a severe fall was the genesis of my career as a sportscaster.

—BOB BARRY

Seven-year-old Bobby Barry's love for strawberry soda pop almost cost him his life on a gorgeous spring day in Oklahoma City in early June, 1938.

The day began when Bobby's older brother, Jack, set up a makeshift pop stand in front of the Barry home on Northwest 26th Street. Jack sold Coca Cola, 7-Up, and orange and grape drinks for five cents, but strawberry was Bobby's favorite. He had used his only nickel to buy a strawberry pop that morning, but was especially thirsty and looked for some way to buy another. His mother was visiting neighbors and his father was at work at his post as secretary-treasurer of Oklahoma City Federal Savings and Loan.

Jack would not sell Bobby a pop on credit, prompting Bobby to call his father to ask permission to borrow a nickel from their next door neighbor, B. Gaylord Noftsger. After Mr. Barry learned Bobby already had consumed one strawberry pop, he said, "No, you cannot ask Mr. Noftsger for a nickel." Bobby lingered around his brother's pop stand for awhile longer and in his mind began to formulate a plan to get the money for a second strawberry pop.[1]

Bobby shrugged off lessons about telling the truth he learned in Sunday school and headed to his neighbor's house. When Mr. Noftsger came to the door, Bobby said, "I called my Daddy and he said I could ask to borrow a nickel from you until he gets home." As a result of Mr. Noftsger's kindness, Bobby ran back home and bought a strawberry pop from his brother.

Unfortunately, Mr. Noftsger came to the Barry home later that evening and laughingly said, "Your kid got a nickel out of me today." Not amused at his youngest son's blatant disobedience, Mr. Barry said to Bobby, "I told you not to borrow money from Mr. Noftsgter." To cover up his first moral error of the day, Bobby lied and responded, "I didn't."

Mr. Barry, who normally had a great sense of humor, was tired and was determined to teach Bobby to tell the truth. He said, "Don't lie to me. Mr. Noftsger told me you borrowed a nickel. Go upstairs!" Bobby was sent to his bedroom without dinner and began crying. His grandmother, Nona Glasgow, affectionately known as "Nanny," tried to comfort him and urged him to go downstairs and admit his disobedience and subsequent lies to his father. Bobby resisted and lay on his bed for what seemed like hours.

After dinner, Bobby heard his mother outside and looked down on the driveway where she was painting a glider swing. Bobby leaned against a window screen to get a better look. Suddenly, the screen latch unhooked and he plunged out the second-story window and landed on his head on the concrete porch below. Inside, Mr. Barry was reading the newspaper in the living room and heard what sounded like "a coconut striking the porch."[2]

Mrs. Barry screamed and ran to Bobby who was bleeding

profusely from every opening in his skull—eyes, mouth, ears, and nose. He did not lose consciousness, but was stunned beyond belief. Mrs. Barry yelled at her husband to get the car. While Bobby's mother and grandmother held him in the back seat with towels draped around his head, Mr. Barry drove at a breakneck speed to Wesley Hospital a few miles from the Barry home. He later told family members, "God must have been looking out for us because I made every green light between home and the hospital." [3]

Before the Barrys left for the hospital, Nanny called famed pediatrician Dr. Carrol Pounders who agreed to meet Bobby at the hospital. [4] Once at Wesley, nurses x-rayed Bobby's head and found that his skull was fractured. Immediately, doctors began assessing the damage. It was encouraging that Bobby was alert, but one doctor said there was a good chance the fall had caused a severe concussion, or even worse, brain damage. A major concern was that gangrene would set in because of the obvious trauma that caused such extensive bleeding. There was such a fear of infection that nurses did not remove Bobby's blood-soaked clothing for three days. [5]

When Bobby Barry fell from the second story of his home in 1938, the incident was reported the following morning in *The Daily Oklahoman*. *Courtesy Oklahoma Publishing Company*.

Screen Gives Way, Boy Breaks Skull

An X-ray picture Wednesday at Wesley hospital revealed Bobby Barry, 7 years old, son of Mr. and Mrs. Jack E. Barry jr., 2716 Northwest Twenty-sixth street, suffered a fractured skull when he fell from a second story window to a concrete porch at his home Tuesday night. The boy was in the window when a screen came unhooked. His father is secretary-treasurer of the Oklahoma City Federal Savings and Loan association.

After doctors evaluated the situation, it was determined that no surgery was needed, but Bobby would be required to lie in bed for eight weeks without lifting his head from the pillow. Both Bobby and his parents were shocked. How could a seven-year-old active boy lie in bed without sitting up for two months?

Carefully, Bobby was taken home to his bedroom and the long period of convalescence began. He could not leave his bed to eat or make trips to the bathroom. Instead, he was served his meals in bed while lying perfectly flat. He used the bathroom in a hospital-type urinal and bedpan.

Bobby's near tragedy was reported the following morning in *The Daily Oklahoman*. The story of his fractured skull appeared in the state's largest and most read newspaper under the headline, "SCREEN GIVES WAY, BOY BREAKS SKULL."[6]

In 1938, television was yet to be available to the general public, so Bobby's days were spent listening to radio. He memorized the names of hosts and performers on radio shows. He was already a sports fan and was intrigued by sports announcers. When the Oklahoma City Indians were playing, Bobby listened to games broadcast on a local radio station. His father had told him that sometimes the announcers were not actually in person in some distant city for away games, but instead recreated the broadcasts at the radio station in Oklahoma City by retrieving the play-by-play results from a news wire and using sound effects.

During the long eight weeks of recovery, Bobby listened to dozens of baseball games. In addition to soaking up every word said by announcers broadcasting the Indians minor league games, he listened to major league baseball games in faraway cities such as St. Louis, Missouri. At night, KMOX Radio's signal boomed into

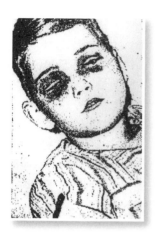

Bobby's photograph appeared in *The Daily Oklahoman* along with the story about him falling from the second story window of his home. *Courtesy Oklahoma Publishing Company.*

Oklahoma City and brought play-by-play coverage of the St. Louis Cardinals into Bobby's bedroom.

Bobby recovered from the effects of the fall. However, when he was allowed to leave his bed after eight weeks, he could not walk—his legs were atrophied. Although he quickly regained his ability to walk and move about like other seven-year-old boys, the severe injury affected his health throughout his adolescent and teenage years.[7]

Perhaps Bobby's intense exposure to radio sportscasters in the summer of 1938 spawned a future career choice unique in Oklahoma history. For more than 50 years, Bob Barry has broadcast more major college sporting events on radio as the play-by-play announcer than anyone else in the annals of sports. Had he not been confined to a bed for almost an entire summer vacation, he may have ended up running a savings and loan like his father. Fortunately for sports fans, his life took a spectacular turn once he sat behind a microphone for the first time.

CHAPTER TWO

A Proud Family Heritage

Our parents were concerned that my brother and I pay attention to preachers and teachers at our church to learn how to live a proper life.

—BOB BARRY

Robert Guyton Barry was born on February 28, 1931, at Wesley Hospital in Oklahoma City. As a child he was called Bobby—later he shortened his name to Bob.

The night before his birth, his mother, Frances Louamma Barry, packed and re-packed her small suitcase for the short trip to the hospital while her husband, John Emmet "Jack" Barry, Jr., made certain their automobile was filled with gasoline. The Barrys knew Oklahoma's weather could change in a swift moment—they were ready to leave for the hospital early if the announcer on the radio in the kitchen predicted another round of snow flurries that had made 1931 an exceptionally cold and snowy winter in the state's capital city.

Wesley Hospital was an imposing structure at Northwest 12th Street and Harvey Avenue that had served the medical needs of Oklahoma City residents since 1910. The facility had expanded to

190 beds and attracted the finest doctors in the area. The Barrys selected Wesley because many of their friends used the hospital and because the physician they had chosen for delivery preferred the staff and equipment at Wesley rather than at nearby Mercy Hospital. Wesley later became Presbyterian Hospital and eventually moved to the Oklahoma Health Center campus south of the State Capitol.[1]

Bob was born without fanfare or incident as Oklahoma prepared for the first of March and much-anticipated better weather. Oklahoma winters had a habit of disappearing quickly and blossoming into budding trees and warmer days as springtime approached. At first, his parents were uncertain what to name him because Frances badly wanted a girl and had not seriously thought of a name for a boy.[2]

The birth certificate from Wesley Hospital listed "Baby Barry." The next day his four-year-old brother, Jack, began calling him "Bob." Frances accepted that recommendation and officially named her son Robert. Family lore does not preserve the story of how Bob's middle name became Guyton, although it perhaps came from a distant cousin of which no record exists.

It was an active world into which Bob was born. In the month before his birth, Thomas Edison submitted his last patent application; Charlie Chaplin's movie, "City Lights," was released; the original film version of "Dracula," starring Bela Lugosi, debuted; and Congress gave the State of California permission to build the San Francisco-Oakland Bay Bridge.[3]

On the day of Bob's birth, future legendary college basketball coach Dean Smith was born in Emporia, Kansas, and Chicago mob boss, Alphonse "Al" Capone, was sentenced to six months in jail for defying a federal judge's order to return from the Bahamas to face criminal charges for "nearly every major crime in Chicago in the last five years."[4]

Three days after Bobby was born, "The Star Spangled Banner" was officially adopted as the United States National Anthem. When Bobby was ten days old, Oklahoma aviator Wiley Post announced he would attempt to fly around the world that summer in his single-engine airplane, the *Winnie Mae*.[5] No pilot had accomplished that gargantuan feat to that time in history.

Even though the young Barry family was excited about having their second child, there was an air of concern in their hometown and the entire nation. The United States was being choked by the Great Depression, the most severe economic downturn in modern history.

Oklahoma suffered greatly in the Great Depression. The misery began when the stock market crashed in October, 1929, and worsened as banks failed, factories and businesses closed, unemployment rolls swelled, and home and farm foreclosures became daily events. In the cities, men stood on street corners looking for work for the day. In rural areas, thousands of tenant farmers gave up on the land and headed for greener pastures in California, a trek immortalized in John Steinbeck's Pulitzer Prize-winning novel *The Grapes of Wrath*.[6]

In addition to economic woes, much of Oklahoma was scorched by a long drought that desiccated even normally wet eastern Oklahoma and birthed dust storms never seen in the young state. Dust blew in such quantities that chickens went to roost at noon, travelers lost their way, airports closed, and trains stopped. When babies were born in areas wracked by dust storms, a wet cloth had to be quickly placed over the infant's mouth and nose to prevent ingestion of swirling dust. Blistering heat accompanied the drought. During the Great Depression some towns in Oklahoma recorded temperatures over 100 degrees for 35 consecutive days.[7]

Oklahoma City was better off than cities and towns in rural Oklahoma. Not long before Bobby's birth, oil had become the password of the Oklahoma City economy. In 1928, oil was discovered in the Oklahoma City field, the first time a major oil field was found inside the city limits of a major American city. Hundreds of jobs were created within a matter of days and the population of the city increased by 10,000 within months.[8]

Even with the positive effects provided by oil field jobs, Jack Barry, Jr., and the Oklahoma City Federal Savings and Loan had difficult times in the early 1930s. Farmers and ranchers in outlying areas could not travel to Oklahoma City to buy from merchants who needed to repay loans from Oklahoma City Federal. The ripple effect was chilling to all. However, it was not the first time that an economic downturn affected the lives of the Barry family.

A previous recession was the primary reason Bobby's paternal and maternal grandparents had moved to Oklahoma City for a fresh start after their businesses failed in Texas. Bobby's paternal grandfather, John Emmet Barry, known as Jack Barry, Sr., was a pharmacist in Paris, the county seat of Lamar County, Texas. Paris was an old town in north Texas, designated as the county seat in 1844 and incorporated in the Republic of Texas in 1845. The town was named for its counterpart in France and became a cattle and farming center.

Jack Barry, Sr. was born in Paris where his father had arrived 40 years earlier as an eight-year-old immigrant from Ireland. Bob's great grandfather, John Emmet Barry, who had the same name as his son, was born in Dublin, Ireland, in the 1840s and was sent to live with relatives in Paris when both his parents died. He made the trip alone across the Atlantic Ocean by boat and then to Texas by train. As he reached adulthood he was a captain in the Confederate Army. After the Civil War, he returned to Paris and married Hattie Johnson.[9]

Jack Barry, Sr., and his wife, Martha Humphries Barry, had one son, John Emmet Barry, known as Jack Barry, Jr., who was born in Paris in 1899. The Barrys owned a popular drug store on the town square in Paris and even dabbled in inventing pharmaceutical products. He developed a particular soap that he claimed could cure freckles on a youngster's face. The product sold well until federal officials made him stop making the soap because one of the main ingredients was banned and he could not scientifically back up claims that freckles disappeared after a month's washing.[10]

The Barry Drug Store did well at first, but then economic problems caused by the Panic of 1896 deflated commodities prices and drove the stock market to new lows. As with other trends, the economic recession did not immediately affect businesses in north Texas. But as markets dried up for Paris-area farmers, Barry's customers could not pay their bills. Barry was a prominent member of the local Disciples of Christ congregation and could not bring himself to press his customers for payment. Without cash to pay his creditors, the business closed.

At about the time of the business failure, there was talk of the United States entering World War I in Europe. For the first two years of fighting, America had taken an isolationist position and tried to broker peace between warring factions. However, when Germany sank the *Lusitania*, killing more than 100 Americans,

President Woodrow Wilson and Congress began taking a longer
look at possible United States involvement. As Congress prepared
to declare war against Germany in 1917, the Barrys and their 18-
year-old son, Jack, Jr., left Paris and settled in Oklahoma City.

Bobby's maternal grandparents also were affected by a bad
economy in north Texas in the early years of the twentieth century.
J. Bachman Glasgow, born in South Carolina, and his wife, Nona
Bond Glasgow, were in the dry goods business in Gainesville,
Texas, the county seat of Cooke County, whose northern boundary
was the Red River. When the dry goods business no longer was
profitable, the Glasgows closed their store and moved to Tishom-
ingo, Oklahoma, where he worked in a dry goods store until they
relocated to Oklahoma City in 1917, along with their only child,
Frances Louamma Glasgow, born in Gainesville in 1900. Frances
graduated from Oklahoma City Central High School in 1918.[11]

Even though the Barrys and Glasgows were not acquainted
in Texas, their move to Oklahoma City ultimately brought their
families together. The Barrys occupied a large house in northeast
Oklahoma City and rented rooms to three young single men, of
which B. Gaylord Noftsger was one. Noftsger was a few years older
than Jack, Jr., but often played tennis with him. When Noftsger was
married, his wife, Clyde, had a young friend, Frances Glasgow,
who she introduced to Jack, Jr. After a brief courtship, Jack, Jr. and
Frances were married in 1923. They later lived next door to the
Noftsgers. Mr. Noftsger was a well-known architect in Oklahoma
City and designed the downtown bus station, the mausoleum at
Rose Hill Cemetery, and numerous housing additions as Oklahoma
City quickly expanded to the northwest.[12]

Jack, Jr. had been working as a traveling adding machine salesman before he was married. Not wanting to be away from home most of the week, he quit his sales job and was hired as a bookkeeper at the Oklahoma City Building and Loan Association, whose name was changed to Oklahoma City Federal Savings and Loan during the New Deal policies of President Franklin D. Roosevelt, that provided federal insurance and protection for depositors of the nation's savings and loans.[13] The Oklahoma City Building and Loan Association was one of Oklahoma City's oldest financial institutions, founded in 1899 with pioneer leader Anton Classen as its first president.[14]

Jack, Jr. had no education beyond high school except for one year at Texas Christian University where he played shortstop on the baseball team and joined the ROTC program. The bookkeeping job at Oklahoma City Building and Loan Association was all he could qualify for at the time. However, wanting to improve himself, he enrolled in night school to obtain a degree, closely observed his superiors at the savings and loan, and learned the lending business. Savings and loans were popular and promoted by the government as a congenial lending source from which American families could

The trolley heading north on Classen Boulevard in 1934. During Bob Barry's childhood, the trolley was a popular form of transportation in Oklahoma City. *Courtesy Oklahoma Heritage Association.*

Bob's father, Jack E. Barry, Jr., began as a bookkeeper at Oklahoma City Federal Savings and Loan and worked his way up to the top as chairman of the institution.

Bob at age two in 1933 in front of the Barry home in Oklahoma City. After his birth, Frances and Jack Barry decided Bob would be the last child in the family.

purchase homes in the boom times of the 1920s.

Jack, Jr. was personable, had a wonderful sense of humor, and was disciplined enough to juggle his workload with his continuing education. On February 12, 1927, Frances had their first child, Jack Glasgow Barry. By the time Bob was born in 1931, Jack, Jr. had been named secretary-treasurer of Oklahoma City Federal and was a member of the thrift's board of directors. Eventually, before his retirement, he became chairman of the board of the savings and loan association that later became Continental Federal Savings and Loan.[15]

The Barry family emphasized religious training for their boys. Jack and Bob were required to attend Sunday school and other functions at Central Presbyterian Church. "We were there every time the doors were open," Bob remembered. "Our parents were concerned that we pay attention to teachers and preachers at our church to learn how to live a proper life." On Sunday nights, Bob and Jack attended Christian Endeavor, a specialized training program for children and youth.[16]

After Bob's brush with death when he fell from the second-story bedroom in 1938, his interest in radio was sparked by a gift from his father. Mr. Barry had been to Chicago on business and returned with a kit that allowed Bob to put on radio shows using a printed script and sound effects.

In addition, Bob had a baseball game set that contained dice and spotter cards. He made a separate card for each major league baseball player and created games involving the players. There was no air conditioning, so neighbors could hear young Bob "announcing" the games each afternoon. It was his first try at "play-by-play." Bob was on his own during playtime because the four years that separated he and his brother caused their interests to be varied. As Jack became a teenager, he played with his friends more and his little brother less.[17]

Bob's early life was greatly influenced by his maternal grandmother, Nona Glasgow, called "Nanny," who was the ninth child in her family. Nanny, who worked for more than 30 years in the baby department at Kerr's Department Store, actually did more of the disciplining in the household than the boys' mother. Nanny had lost her husband in 1925 and moved in with her daughter and son-in-law before either Jack or Bob were born.

"Nanny really raised us," Bob remembered. "Mother was a nice sweet lady but did not have the patience to keep up with two growing boys. It was Nanny who set us straight when we needed talking to." [18]

Jack and Bob's father, "a very proper man," played a strong support role in their lives and taught them about money, responsibility, and manners. "He was a fantastic man," Jack remembered, "He was always positive, but strict in his rules and punishment." Once when Jack was a teenager and came in drunk from a party, he crashed in his bedroom. When he awoke, his father was sitting beside the bed reading the newspaper. Without any anger or frustration in his voice, Mr. Barry said, "You feel bad? I guess you shouldn't go to any more parties! That's final." Jack's days of attending teen-

ABOVE: Bob was three years old in 1934.
His mother, Frances, won $50 for this
photograph in a competition at the
Oklahoma State Fair.

RIGHT: Jack Barry, Jr., and his two sons,
Bob, in front, and Jack Glasgow Barry, in
1934. Bob was three and Jack was seven.
Courtesy Jack Glasgow Barry.

age parties where there was drinking were over.[19]

For the first years of Bob's life, the family lived on Northwest 15th Street near Classen High School. Mr. Barry built a room onto the house for Nanny. She lived with them for decades until she died in 1962 at age 88.

Bob began his formal education in kindergarten at Gatewood Elementary School. Soon after, his father received a promotion at work and built a new house on Northwest 26th Street two blocks from Taft Stadium. It was "out in the country" with only three houses on the block. There was a huge field and ponds to the north, "a wilderness" for Bob and his friends.[20]

Because of the move, Bob attended grade school at Cleveland Elementary School. He was a "sickly child." Having never fully recovered from the head injury, he had worse cases of normal childhood illnesses than his friends. He nearly died once with pneumonia and could not concentrate in school. To this day, he has trouble reading a book from cover to cover.[21]

Bob often visited his paternal grandparents, "Daddy Pop" and "Nanny Barry," who lived in a nearby apartment. Nanny Barry was known as a great cook. Especially at holiday time, the family requested she cook her famous roast on a fireless cooker, a newfangled invention that heated concrete discs upon which the meat was placed to roast all day. "The roast would melt in your mouth," Jack remembered.[22]

Daddy Pop and Nanny Barry frequented Oklahoma City Indian baseball games. Nanny Barry's great uncle was Jimmie Humphries, part owner of the Oklahoma City Indians. Because of the family relationship, Bob's grandparents received free tickets to Indians home games played at Holland Field at Northwest Fourth Street and

Pennsylvania Avenue. Oklahoma City joined the Texas League in 1933 and the ballpark became known as Texas League Park.[23]

In 1941, when Bob was ten years old, the Oklahoma City Indians became the top farm club of the Cleveland Indians. Bob seldom missed a home game as future major league stars Thurman Tucker, Jim Hegan, Dixie Howell, Eddie Lopat, and Bill Voiselle played for the local club. In 1940 and 1941, the great Hall of Famer Rogers Hornsby was field manager for the Indians.[24]

From an early age, Bob was drawn to music. His father played piano by ear and "could get all over the piano on ragtime stuff." When Bob was ten, he received a drum set for Christmas. Mr. Barry later admitted he wanted to see if Bob "had rhythm or not." He recognized that some people had rhythm—others did not.

Bob practiced playing the drums often, much to the chagrin of neighbors listening through open windows. However, in his teenage years, Bob put his ability on drums to work. He played with his father at Rotary and Kiwanis clubs and school assemblies. During World

Bob plays drums while his father plays piano at a Rotary Club meeting at Oklahoma City's Biltmore Hotel during World War II.

LEFT: Bob's uncle, Jimmie Humphries, right, part owner of the Oklahoma City Indians minor league baseball club, with Indians manager Jimmy Tatum. The family relationship resulted in free tickets to Indians home games for Bob and his family. *Courtesy Oklahoma Publishing Company.*

RIGHT: Al "Flip" Rosen was one of Bob's favorite Oklahoma City Indian baseball players of the 1940s. After playing minor league baseball in Oklahoma City, Rosen became a star for the Cleveland Indians, winning the American League Most Valuable Player award in 1953. He later was president of the New York Yankees, the Houston Astros, and the San Francisco Giants. *Courtesy Oklahoma Publishing Company.*

War II, they played ragtime for workers at Tinker Air Force Base.

Bob attended junior high school at Taft Junior High where he joined the national junior high school fraternity, Pi Kappa Pi. Through the fraternity, he made lasting friendships. At Taft, during World War II, budget cuts prevented competitive sports competition, but Bob tried out for the baseball team at Classen High School when he enrolled there. He lettered in baseball at Classen and played with friends such as Lee Allan Smith. Bob pitched and played in the outfield. Smith, the shortstop, said, "Nobody loved baseball better than Bob." [25] Fifty years later, when the two old friends meet, strangers are intrigued with their back and forth banter recalled from high school days, "Home baby, home boy." [26] Bob had enjoyed being a member of a fraternity at Taft, so he joined Phi Lamda Epsilon, another national fraternity, at Classen.

Bob played American Legion baseball for the Fred Jones Ford team. Once when the team played in far south Oklahoma City at Capitol Hill High School, he missed his ride home and began walking. His parents thought he had been kidnapped because the trip on foot took several hours. When a neighbor offered to give him a ride for the final block, Bob responded, "No, I think I'll just finish the trip myself." [27]

Bob could not get enough of baseball. He especially enjoyed springtime exhibition games when major league teams appeared in Oklahoma City before the regular baseball season began. While Bob was in high school, he became a huge fan of Al Rosen who played for the Oklahoma City Indians. In 1947, Rosen almost rewrote the Texas League record book. He led the league in batting, hits, doubles, and runs batted in and was the league Most Valuable Player.

Because Bob was interested in sportscasting, he listened to Oklahoma City Indian games when he was not at the ballpark in person. He was in awe of young Curt Gowdy who became the radio voice of the Indians. Gowdy was hired by Bob's uncle to broadcast Indian games on KOCY Radio, a 250-watt radio station. The Indians could not pay Gowdy at first, but he lined up advertisers to pay his salary. The home games were broadcast live, but Gowdy had to recreate road games with the help of Western Union. Gowdy said:

I selected a block of wood with a small stick. When it came
across the wire that a batter had hit the ball, I struck the block

with my stick. I secured a large photo of every Texas League park so I could visualize "being there."

The telegrapher would type out the report for the visiting ball park. B1 was ball one. S2 was strike two. He would use "single to right" or "double to left." I let my imagination soar, and it was valuable training for my ad-lib ability.[28]

Bob listened intently to Gowdy's broadcasts of Indian games. He also listened to a variety of sporting events, from boxing to football. Even then, he was formulating phrases and colorful descriptions that would benefit him during a half-century career as a sportscaster.

BELOW: Two of Bob's teenage heroes were Oklahoma City Indians broadcaster Curt Gowdy, left, and Cleveland Indians pitcher Bob Feller. Gowdy interviews Feller before a 1947 exhibition game at Texas League Park in Oklahoma City. *Courtesy Oklahoma Publishing Company.*

ABOVE: Bob attended junior high at Taft Junior High School in northwest Oklahoma City.

Gowdy, who married an Oklahoma City girl, Jerre Dawkins, while he worked at KOCY Radio and KOMA Radio where he broadcast University of Oklahoma football games and Oklahoma A & M basketball. After leaving Oklahoma City, Gowdy became one of America's most respected and enduring sportscasters. He was the longtime voice of the Boston Red Sox and the lead announcer for NBC Television in early coverage of the American Football League and the baseball Game of the Week on Saturday afternoons.[29]

At the Texas League Park, Bob also met Indians announcer Bob Murphy who later broadcast games for the Boston Red Sox and Baltimore Orioles before becoming the first announcer for the New York Mets. Murphy was an Oklahoman whose first appearance in a broadcast booth was with the minor league Muskogee, Oklahoma Reds. Both Murphy and Gowdy later were inducted into the broadcasting division of the National Baseball Hall of Fame.[30]

In high school, Bob played on the Fred Jones Ford American Legion team. Left to right, Bob, Bob Waller, and Bud Bergthold.

Bob's talent as a high school pitcher brought him a few minutes of fame with the Oklahoma City Indians. He was asked by Indians manager Joe Vosmik, at the suggestion of Bob's uncle and team owner Jimmie Humphries, to pitch batting practice and was provided an Indians uniform. Bob remembered, "I thought I was Mr. Stud." When Bob's brother saw him signing an autograph after batting practice, a rumor began to circulate that Bob was a regular pitcher for the Indians.[31]

Bob was envied by good friends such as Ralph Thompson, who remembered, "We couldn't believe this tall, skinny kid was in an Indians uniform on the mound while we sat in the bleachers. We were truly awed by him getting to be on the same field with our childhood baseball heroes." [32]

On another occasion after pitching batting practice, Bob locked the keys in his car, an old Chevrolet coupe he had purchased with the help of his father. Not able to get into the car, Bob called his father who promptly brought a second set of keys from the Barry home to the ballpark. Bob retrieved his change of clothing from the car and accidentally locked the second set of keys inside the vehicle. He was embarrassed and had to call his father again. This time, his mother met Mr. Barry in the driveway. When he returned to the ballpark, he looked at Bob and said, "Damn, son!" It was one of the few times Bob ever heard his father say anything close to a curse word. After the use of a coat hanger, Bob was able to drive home.[33]

During the summer before his senior year in high school, Bob worked as a mail clerk at KOMA Radio located in the Biltmore Hotel in downtown Oklahoma City. The station had begun broadcasting on Christmas Eve in 1922 using the call letters KFJF. In 1932, the station became KOMA and was licensed by the Federal Communications Commission to broadcast with 50,000 watts, making it one of the most powerful radio stations west of the Mississippi River. The mail room where Bob worked was near the broadcast studios, so Bob saw the behind-the-scenes production of local programs and the interaction of KOMA and the CBS Radio Network.

Bob graduated from Classen High School in 1949 and enrolled at the University of Oklahoma (OU) in Norman. His college career was anything but a success. His learning and concentration struggles that had begun in the classroom in high school continued in college. He skipped classes frequently and "went bananas" perhaps because his father had been so strict in high school. Mr. Barry gave him $500 to cover expenses for the first year, but Bob was broke by December 1 of the first semester. From that time, Mr. Barry said he was forced to treat Bob "like a baby" and sent him a weekly allowance.[34]

Bob joined the Kappa Alpha fraternity and spent more time socializing than studying. His grades were poor, much to the chagrin of his father and his fraternity pledge trainer, Don Symcox, who had arrived at OU and the Kappa Alpha house from his hometown of Cordell, Oklahoma. Symcox remembered, "My first impression of Bob was not good. He had no interest in studying or going to the library. It was a chore to get him to sit down long enough to look at a book for more than 10 minutes."[35]

Symcox, who later became one of Bob's closest lifelong friends, also was annoyed by Bob interrupting other students' studies at the fraternity house. "He and his group of friends were always involved in weird antics like trying to move around a room without walking on the floor," Symcox said. Bob entertained Kappa Alpha house residents by making up baseball games and doing the play-by-play to entertain students who gathered around him.[36]

Bob also had problems handling money. He bounced checks, causing his brother, a member of another fraternity, to call their father with the emergency message, "Dad, his checks are bouncing and they are calling me!"[37]

After two years at OU, Bob changed his major from drama to economics, but his academic performance did not improve. The admissions office informed him in 1951 that his grades were not good enough to earn a deferment from the Selective Service draft for the Korean War. Deferments were available only for students in the upper two-thirds of a college class. When Bob told his father that he was near the bottom of his class, Mr. Barry said, "What branch of the military are you going to join?"[38]

Bob had two choices—be drafted by the United States Army and be trained as an infantryman, or join the United States Air Force. He chose the latter.

CHAPTER THREE

Marriage, The Air Force, and a New Career

Marrying Joan was the best thing that had ever happened in my life.
—BOB BARRY

Bob's decision to join the Air Force was totally driven by the Korean War that had begun in June, 1950, when North Korea invaded South Korea. The United States and the United Nations intervened on the side of South Korea and the American military began drafting soldiers for the conflict. Even though Congress never officially declared war, the "police action" nevertheless cost American lives for three years in fighting that involved trench warfare, swift infantry attacks, and air bombing raids.

Bob was not destined to spend his Air Force career alone. In college, his grandmother had encouraged him to date Joan Hester, a beautiful young girl in his Sunday school class at St. Andrews Presbyterian Church. Bob was president and Joan was vice president of the class. When Bob called Joan, her mother answered, and to his disappointment, Joan was not at home. Ten days later, Bob called again, and this time Joan accepted Bob's invitation for a date. Bob remembered, "As luck would have it, my car stalled in her driveway and people thought it was a set up deal." Later Joan admitted she had a crush on Bob even before his first call.[1]

Bob and Joan, the daughter of James and Ruth Hester, "hit it off great" and fell in love. After a few months of dating, they talked about marriage. Bob also won the heart of his future mother-in-law by buying her an orchid on Mother's Day, 1952. Mrs. Hester wrote:

We are very happy about you and Joan…Mothers are supposed to be sad about giving their daughters in marriage (and Joan and I have been closer than most mothers and daughters) but you two are so right for each other and your wonderful family are so kind to her in every way, I can't be sad. We love you and I know everything will be perfect for you two super people.[2]

Wedding plans were temporarily delayed when Bob received notice from the Air Force to report for active duty. After dinner at Beverly's Restaurant one night, Bob kissed Joan and his family

Joan Hester visiting relatives in San Diego, California, in 1938. She was six years old.

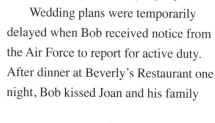

Joan Hester's father was Colonel James Raymond Hester who spent most of World War II in a Japanese concentration camp. He was captured in China and was freed only after the war ended with the defeat of the Japanese.

Bob and Joan washing his car in the Hester driveway in 1951.

goodbye and boarded a train for basic training at Lackland Air Force Base in San Antonio, Texas.

With six weeks training completed, Bob was assigned as a teacher in the Supply School at Francis E. Warren Air Force Base (Warren AFB) in Cheyenne, Wyoming. It was the first time Bob had been to Wyoming and he feared the long winters of which his friends in Oklahoma had warned him.[3]

Warren AFB, named for Wyoming's first governor, had a long and illustrious history. Within days of his arrival, Bob learned that the base was the oldest continuously active military installation in the Air Force. The base was opened in 1867 as Fort David A. Russell, named in honor of a Civil War general. The first cavalry troops stationed there lived in tents. In 1930, President Herbert Hoover changed the name of the post to Fort Warren.

During World War II, Fort Warren was the training center for 20,000 troops of the Quartermaster Corps. Nearly 300 wooden buildings were built without insulation to house the influx of trainees. In the harsh Wyoming winter, waking up in the barracks often meant shaking snow from one's blanket before heading for the cold communal showers. In 1947, four years before Bob was stationed there, Fort Warren was transferred to the Air Force and became

Warren AFB.

During orientation, Bob discovered that Warren AFB had been home to a number of famous soldiers, including Dr. Walter Reed; General Mark Clark; General Benjamin O. Davis, the first American black general; General Billy Mitchell, the "father of the Air Force;" and superstar Sammy Davis, Jr. Entertainer Neil Diamond grew up at the installation while his father was assigned to the base.

After a few weeks of teaching classes each day for airmen training for the Air Force Supply Service, Bob called Joan and asked her to plan a wedding. He simply could no longer exist without her at his side in Wyoming. He flew home to Oklahoma City and they were married at St. Andrews Presbyterian Church on December 27, 1952. Bob was 21, Joan was 19. They spent their honeymoon in Tulsa and then drove back to Cheyenne.[4]

The Air Force was good for Bob. He had not done well academically in college and needed time away from his parents. In his words, "It was time I grew up." With a new wife and new responsibilities, growing up came quickly. It came even swifter when Joan announced she was pregnant. Their first son, John Franklin "Frank" Barry, was born at the Warren AFB hospital on April 6, 1954. The Barrys' personal cost for delivery was $12.

Air Force pay did not provide the Barrys with a luxurious lifestyle. He said, "One week, we lived on Bisquick with everything from pancakes to waffles to biscuits with gravy." Bob renewed his friendship with Classen High School buddy Lee Thompson, Jr., who was a first lieutenant stationed at Warren AFB. Bob was a staff sergeant and Thompson never has allowed him to forget he outranked him, at least for their time in the Air Force.[5]

Thompson and his wife, Ann, became constant companions of

Bob and Joan were married at St. Andrews Presbyterian Church in Oklahoma City on December 27, 1952, by Reverend W.A. Bennett.

When Bob married Joan in 1952, his brother Jack, left, was his best man.

Bob and Joan wave at well-wishers as they leave their wedding in December, 1952.

Bob and Joan at their wedding reception at St. Andrews Presbyterian Church.

ABOVE: At Bob and Joan's 1952 wedding in Oklahoma City were his parents, at left, Jack and Frances Barry, and Joan's mother, Ruth Philpin and step-father John Philpin.

When Bob was married in 1952, three of his four grandparents remained alive. Left to right, Martha Barry, John E. "Jack" Barry, Sr., and Nona Glasgow.

Bob and Joan. Thompson remembered, "We spent many hours playing Monopoly in the Barrys' basement apartment. During the day when we could slip away from our offices, Bob and I would play ping pong for hours." [6]

For four years, Bob served in the Air Force and was never stationed anywhere but Warren AFB. When teachers were being reassigned to Korea, he transferred to the evaluation section and spent his days grading trainees' examination papers.

Bob and Joan with two-week old John Franklin "Frank" Barry, their first child, in 1954. At the time, Bob was on active duty in the United States Air Force at Warren Air Force Base in Cheyenne, Wyoming. Frank was born at 6:00 a.m. on April 6, 1954, and weighed eight pounds two ounces.

Bob was discharged from the Air Force in late 1955 and the young Barry family returned to Norman. They moved into apartment number three at 1012 Classen Avenue. Bob wanted to return to school, but he also had a family to support. He played in a dance band on weekends and landed a job in 1956 as a radio advertising salesman at KNOR Radio in Norman.

Bob's musical talents allowed to him to earn extra money when he was discharged from the Air Force and moved his young family to Norman. He sits at his parents' piano where he proposed to Joan.

When Bob began selling radio advertising at KNOR Radio in 1956, his first account was Goodno's Jewelry on East Main Street in Norman. He interviews Mrs. Goodno during a remote broadcast.

KNOR had been on the air since 1949 and was managed by William "Bill" Morgan. KNOR owner Tol Dickinson had won a bidding war with the *Norman Transcript* for the license of Norman's second radio station. The Federal Communications Commission was concerned about the city's newspaper also owning a radio station and awarded the license to Dickinson. While Bob worked at the radio station, Joan took a job as a secretary at Oklahoma Gas and Electric Company.[7]

Bob was given the job at KNOR because of his father's influence. Jack Barry's friend, Ray Wilson, was a salesman at KTOK Radio in Oklahoma City and gave Bob a short course in how to sell radio time. Wilson called Morgan at KNOR and said, "You must give this young man a chance. He needs a job now!"[8]

Bob surprised himself by making better grades in his second try at college. However, he liked radio so much that he told Joan one night he did not need any more education and had found his lifelong career. He dropped out of school, played as many dance band gigs as he could, and worked at KNOR.

Sales came natural to Bob. When he was a child he had won

Bob's brother, Jack, right, married Barbara Bizzell, the granddaughter of former University of Oklahoma President William Bennett Bizzell, in 1950 in New Orleans, Louisiana. Jack graduated from OU the same year with a degree in political science and spent 45 years in the insurance business in Oklahoma and North Carolina. He and Barbara had three children. *Courtesy Jack Glasgow Barry.*

Robert Bonnin Barry, known to the broadcasting world as Bob Barry, Jr., and to the family as "Bobby," on his first birthday in 1957. He was born in Norman on December 21, 1956, at Norman Municipal Hospital and weighed six pounds six ounces. He was named for his father and his great grandfather, Leo Samuel Bonnin. The Barrys lived at 205 West Haddock when Bobby joined the Barry family.

awards for selling more magazines than other students in his class. "My brother couldn't sell anything," Bob said, "but I sold like mad. The good Lord gave me something to be able to convince people to buy whatever I was selling." [9]

In addition to selling advertising to Norman businesses, Bob debuted with an early morning radio show, "Uncle Bob's Wake Up Jamboree." KNOR was off the air from midnight to 6:15 a.m. when Bob began his morning broadcast. Each morning long before day-light, Bob arose, dressed, and picked up a cup of coffee at a local restaurant as he headed to the radio station on East Alameda Street on the east side of Norman. Bob was a slight bit intimidated by be-ing on the air. He nervously tapped his pencil during his first hour on the air, prompting the engineer to tell him the audience could hardly hear him above the pencil tapping. [10]

The Barry family grew with the birth of a second son, Robert

Bobby Barry, left, and his big brother, Frank, in 1957. Frank was two years old when Bobby was born.

Frank Barry in the first grade in 1959.

Bonnin "Bobby" Barry, at Norman Municipal Hospital on December 21, 1956. Later known in the broadcast world as "Bob Barry, Jr." to distinguish him from his father, Bobby was named for his father and his maternal great grandfather, Leo Samuel Bonnin.

Bob actually missed Bobby's birth at the hospital. At the moment he was born, Bob was at Owen Field interviewing legendary running back Jim Brown. Brown was the star of the 1956 Syracuse University football squad that was preparing to play in the Cotton Bowl in Dallas on New Year's Day. Syracuse coach Ben Swartzwalder was a friend of OU coach Bud Wilkinson who allowed the Syracuse team to use OU facilities, including Owen Field, in preparation for their bowl game.[11]

Jack Ogle also worked at KNOR and was the play-by-play announcer for Norman High School football and basketball games. Soon Ogle left KNOR for a similar announcing position at WNAD

Radio, a Norman station owned by OU, with studios in the Oklahoma Memorial Union. As the 1957 football season approached, General Manager Morgan asked Bob, "Can you do play-by-play?" Having done play-by-play in his bedroom since he was a child, Bob said, "Sure I can." That Friday night, Bob did his first football broadcast and began a sportscasting career that has lasted for more than a half century.[12]

Bob received early instruction on play-by-play from OU student Ross Porter. Porter was the son of the newspaper publisher in Shawnee and had broadcast high school basketball games on KGFF Radio in his hometown. KNOR manager Morgan called Porter at the Sigma Alpha Epsilon fraternity house and asked him to do the play-by-play for Norman High basketball games and to allow Bob to sit with him to "learn the business." Porter and Bob broadcast the Tiger basketball games from inside a soundproof, glass booth that was placed on the floor level behind one of the goals in the Norman High gymnasium. Porter remembered, "We learned the hard way. It was spooky not hearing any crowd noise."[13]

Later, Porter broadcast Los Angeles Dodgers games for 28 seasons and was a lead announcer for NBC Sports for decades, including broadcasts of professional football and the World Series. His most famous national call was Game Six of the 1977 World Series when Reggie Jackson hit three home runs. Porter holds the record for broadcasting 22 consecutive innings in a 1989 Los Angeles-Houston baseball game and is the only broadcaster to be the voice of a World Series champion, Los Angeles, and the national collegiate basketball champion, the University of Nevada at Las Vegas.[14]

Getting reestablished in Norman, Bob discovered his Kappa Alpha pledge trainer, Don Symcox, had married Mary Louise Lee, the daughter of former Oklahoma United States Senator Josh Lee. Symcox had not seen Bob since he left for the Air Force and was shocked when Bob appeared at his apartment door one evening wanting a bottle of bourbon for a party. Oklahoma was a dry state at the time and liquor was not available for retail sale. Fortunately for Bob, Symcox had a bottle stashed away and loaned it his friend. When Bob left, Mary Louise said, "Now, who is that? Why would he show up wanting whiskey? Do you really know him?" [15]

College football was king in Norman. OU head football coach Bud Wilkinson had arrived in 1947 and began to have unprecedented success on the gridiron. In 1949, the Sooners were undefeated and shutout Louisiana State University in the Sugar Bowl; they were denied a national championship that was awarded to Notre Dame, a team that did not play in a bowl game. There were no Associated Press or United Press International polls released after the regular season, so the national champion was crowned before bowl games.

Wilkinson led OU to its first national football championship in 1950. OU football was becoming so popular that university President George L. Cross told the Oklahoma legislature that he was trying to build a university "that the football team could be proud of." In 1952, OU had its first Heisman Trophy winner, Billy Vessels. [16]

In 1953, OU opened the season with a loss to Notre Dame and tied the University of Pittsburgh the following week. The Sooners would not lose another game for more than three years when they were defeated by Notre Dame 7-0 in November, 1957. The 47-game winning streak is a college football record that perhaps will never be broken. In the middle of the streak, OU won back-to-back national championships in 1955 and 1956. Wilkinson teams went 12 consecutive seasons without a conference loss, a major college record that has never been seriously threatened.[17]

In the fall of 1956, Wilkinson broke another barrier. Prentice Gautt, an honor student and senior class president at Douglass High School in Oklahoma City, enrolled at OU without a football scholarship. To that time, no black student ever had been given an athletic scholarship at OU. At first, a group of prominent Oklahoma City doctors and pharmacists created a scholarship fund. However, Wilkinson saw what Gautt could do on the football field and gave him a four-year scholarship.[18]

Author J. Brent Clark, a well-known OU football historian, wrote:

On game days in Norman, everything stopped for almost three hours as these autumn rituals were enacted. Bits and pieces of the football radio broadcasts wafted through open windows and doorways of homes and shops along deserted streets. Almost everyone was caught up under the mystical spell of Wilkinson's Sooners. Young boys in county seat communities desperately wanted to identify with these strong masculine young men who were perceived as true champions.[19]

It was not only young boys who were caught up in OU football. Older men, struggling to succeed in the post-war economy, faithfully attended games at Owen Field, and the elderly tuned in to radio broadcasts with the play-by-play handled by sports director Bill Bryan of KTOK Radio in Oklahoma City.

Bob did not know Wilkinson well, but he knew his sons, Pat and Jay, through Norman High School football and basketball and the Jaycees sandlot baseball team for which Bob served as business manager.

Pat Wilkinson suffered five football injuries at Norman High

School and each time underwent surgery by Dr. Don O'Donoghue, the OU team physician. Pat was so familiar with surgery, he developed an interest in medicine and became a prominent retinal surgeon in Baltimore, Maryland.[20]

Bob knew Jay Wilkinson best because he played at Norman High School until his graduation in 1961. Norman had an excellent basketball program coached by Chet Bryan. The Tigers won a state basketball championship in 1960. Coach Wilkinson did not bother his sons' high school coaches. After the 1960 championship season, Bryan said the Wilkinsons were the only parents he had not heard from that year.[21]

Bob spent much of the year on the road calling Norman High football and basketball games. The high school football season ran from September to December and the basketball season was not completed until February. Norman played other high schools in central Oklahoma, so Bob loaded up his car with broadcasting equipment and traveled to distant stadiums and gymnasiums, hoping that Southwestern Bell Telephone Company had installed a telephone line in the press box for his live broadcast on KNOR.[22]

One of the most exciting high school football games Bob broadcast was the 1960 state championship contest between Norman and Northwest Classen High School. Norman lost the game 16-14, largely because of a controversial play. The Norman quarterback was Jay Wilkinson. Northwest Classen's quarterback, Mike Miller, lateraled to his fullback, Walt Lawson. Wilkinson picks up the story:

> *When the ball hit the ground, some of the officials called it an incomplete pass, and both teams started back to their huddles. One official, who hearsay has it was Miller's uncle,*

hollered, "Pick up the ball, Walt. You can run. It's a lateral."
Lawson scooped it up and ran 69 yards for a touchdown. Be-
cause both teams believed the ball was dead, the game cameras
had been shut off, so there's no game film of this unusual play,
but local sportswriters said it would be talked about for years,
and it was.[23]

Bob actually missed most of the play. After he, fans in the
stands, and opposition players on the field thought the play was
over, Bob looked down at his scorebook to record the incomplete
pass. He looked up and saw Miller scoring. Later, Bob confirmed
that the official was Miller's uncle.[24]

It was not a pretty sight that night in the locker room because
Norman backfield coach Wray Littlejohn, who was so angry about
the controversial call, broke down the locker room door with a
single forearm blow. The oldest Wilkinson son, Pat, was home from
college at Stanford University and interrupted Bob and sportswriters during post-game interviews by insisting in a very loud voice
that the game be forfeited.[25]

While Norman High football and basketball scored great suc-
cesses in the late 1950s, OU football fortunes soured somewhat.
In 1958, the National Collegiate Athletic Association (NCAA)
announced OU was under investigation for alleged violations that
included use of a slush fund to pay for potential recruits to visit
Norman. The controversy centered on Oklahoma City accountant
Art Wood who kept books for The Touchdown Club of Oklahoma,
a prominent group of state business and political leaders, who were
interested in making and keeping OU a perennial football power.
Ultimately, the NCAA placed OU on probation.[26]

With Wilkinson's attention distracted by the NCAA investigation, OU slipped to 7-3 in 1959, the first time a Wilkinson team at OU had lost three games. The 1960 season was a disaster, by OU standards. It was Wilkinson's only losing season at OU with a record of 3-6-1.[27]

There also was trouble brewing in regard to broadcasting OU football games. For many years, any radio station could broadcast games live and the university received no compensation. In the 1950s, four Oklahoma City and two Tulsa radio stations sent crews to Norman and other sites of away games to broadcast the play-by-play to their listeners.

However, in an attempt to gain income for OU, Wilkinson convinced the OU Board of Regents to make a deal with a New York City entrepreneur, Jerry Johnson, for exclusive rights to OU football broadcasts. OU was paid by Johnson who received his revenue by enlisting Texaco Oil Company as the primary sponsor of the games. Local affiliate stations paid Johnson for the right to air the games but could make money by selling advertising for a certain number of "local" spots during the broadcasts.

After the 1960 season, Johnson, Wilkinson, and several members of The Touchdown Club and the OU Athletic Council were unhappy with Bill Bryan's broadcasts of Sooner football games. The Athletic Council announced an open competition for a new play-by-play announcer—a new voice of the OU Sooners.

Fourteen men, including Bob, at age 30, tried out for the announcing job during the OU Varsity/Alumni game in the spring that matched current players with alumni, many of whom were playing in the NFL. Each of the auditioners sat in a different booth atop Owen Field and did the play-by-play for a quarter of the spring game. Bob asked his old friend, Lee Thompson, Jr., to serve as spotter for the audition. It was Thompson's job to point out the players involved in a particular play while Bob described the action. "We were pretty nervous, but very excited about the tryout," Thompson remembered.[28]

Bob had no close relationship with Wilkinson who knew Bob primarily through listening to him broadcast his sons' football and basketball games on KNOR. Often Wilkinson was busy preparing for an OU game and could not attend his sons' games.[29]

Among the other announcers auditioning for the job were Len Morton and John Henry of Tulsa and Jack Ogle and Ross Porter of Oklahoma City. Ogle was a pioneer radio and television news anchor and sports announcer. Porter was sports director at WKY-TV.

At the end of the audition, Coach Wilkinson called Bob and told him he would be the new play-by-play announcer for the 1961 season. For Bob, it was "the biggest thrill" of his professional life.[30]

As consolation to Bill Bryan for losing the play-by-play job, the OU Athletic Council named him producer of the football broadcasts and color commentator to sit alongside Bob in the broadcast booth.

CHAPTER FOUR

Voice of the Sooners

Bob worked hard at being the best play-by-play announcer in the land. He studied the teams and developed a strong system for just telling what was happening on the field—no frills, just the facts.

—LEE THOMPSON, JR.

As the play-by-play announcer of OU football and basketball, Bob was initiated into an exclusive fraternity of sports announcers identified with a college or university to the extent they were called the "voice" of the particular institution.

Radio sportscasting was not a new profession in 1961. Radio had an incredible impact on sports in the first half of the twentieth century. As radio stations went on the air in large cities and small towns, fans no longer had to attend local sporting events to be able to support their teams. They could tune in for the local announcer's live description of the event.[1]

The first sporting event broadcast live on radio was the Jack Dempsey-Bill Miske prizefight, aired on WWJ Radio in Detroit, Michigan, on September 6, 1920. The first radio play-by-play broadcast of a collegiate football game occurred two months later on November 25, 1920, when WTAW Radio in College Station,

Texas, broadcast the game between the University of Texas and Texas A & M University.[2]

Radio established a unique connection between the broadcaster and the audience that did not exist when television became the primary source for live sporting events, especially on the college and professional level. Former major league baseball player and long-time announcer Bob Uecker said he liked radio better than television because, "You can paint a picture in the mind. It's a kick to make baseball come alive to a guy hundreds of miles away who's never even seen your home park."[3]

College football games produced a big impact on early radio. During the Great Depression, game attendance declined and many colleges banned live broadcasts of games, fearing stadiums would be empty as fans stayed home to listen on the radio. By the end of 1935, all conferences had lifted bans on broadcasting games, although the trend was for institutions to sell the exclusive rights for broadcasts as a new source of revenue.

The play-by-play announcer is the primary speaker, valued for his articulate description of the events of a fast-moving sporting event. The color commentator supplements the factual play-by-play description with insight and analysis. When Bob became the voice of the Sooners, professional announcers normally were hired as color commentators. Twenty years later, in the 1980s, former athletes and coaches became more prominent as color commentators, although former OU coach Bud Wilkinson was one of the early successful "non-professional announcer" color commentators in the 1960s. Today, nearly all color commentators are former athletes or coaches.

Bob also joined an exclusive group of play-by-play announcers of OU football. Announcers who previously had broadcast OU football games included Walter Cronkite and Curt Gowdy. By 1961, both were nationally-known figures in broadcasting.

Cronkite had worked for WKY Radio in Oklahoma City early in his career and broadcast OU games in 1936. He changed to the news side of broadcasting and anchored the "CBS Evening News" and became perhaps the most-trusted news commentator in broadcasting history. By 1961, Gowdy was the voice of the Boston Red Sox and lead announcer for NBC Television's broadcasts of the American Football League.

Even though Bob became an instant celebrity as the voice of the Sooners, he did not get rich from broadcasting Sooner games. He was paid $100 per game for the 1961 season.

Bob, right, with Bill Bryan, left, and OU football coach Bud Wilkinson in 1961. Bob replaced Bryan as the voice of the football Sooners in 1961 although Bryan served as Bob's color commentator for the season.

Bob learned much of the information about the Sooners for the upcoming season from longtime OU Sports Information Director (SID) Harold Keith. Having been hired at OU by athletic director Bennie Owen in 1930, Keith was a fixture at OU and was considered to be the ultimate authority on OU athletics. Author Jay C. Upchurch said, "His job was to record and dispense information relating to OU sporting events, but Keith did much more. His sense of history and articulate nature were legendary."[4]

Bob and Keith became close friends. Keith was a pioneer in the sports information business at universities and lived through a great deal of OU sports history. He also was an award-winning author, winning the Newbery Medal in 1958 for his historical novel, *Rifles for Watie*. Keith remained SID until 1969 when he was succeeded by his son, John Keith.

Bob could hardly sleep the week before his first game as voice of the Sooners in September, 1961. It was much more than just a game, it was OU versus Notre Dame at South Bend, Indiana. Bob said, "Talk about a debut! It was scary enough to broadcast a major college football game, much less travel to the storied Notre Dame campus. I was scared to death!"[5] He asked Lee Thompson, Jr., to be his spotter for the game in South Bend, an assignment that continued for many years.

On the morning of the game, Bob's nerves were so bad that SID Keith walked him around the campus to calm him down. Unfortunately, OU lost badly to the Irish. After the game, Bob called his father back in Oklahoma City and asked, "How did I do?" Mr. Barry responded, "You did good, son."[6]

Bob had to be in decent shape to broadcast the OU games. Immediately after each contest, he grabbed a huge tape recorder and headed to the locker room to interview players and coaches. It was long before live interviews were technically possible. While the color commentator reviewed the game and gave final statistics, Bob taped locker room interviews and ran back to the press box to play the interviews on the live broadcast. Often Bob interviewed players while they stood naked in front of their lockers.

Bob's schedule was hectic during the football season. He broadcast Norman High games on Friday night, the OU varsity games on Saturday afternoons, and the OU freshman games on Monday night. In those days, freshmen were not allowed to play on the varsity squad but instead played their own schedule of games. OU lost its first five games of the 1961 season, and fans were restless. "Bud Wilkinson has seen his day," some cried. Bob remembered, "It was the old problem of 'What have you done for me lately?'" A small, but vocal segment of the OU fans quickly had forgotten that Wilkinson had put OU on the football map and the Sooners were the most successful college football program of the previous 20 years."[7]

One of the first five losses was to the Texas Longhorns, 28-7. After the game, senior co-captain Billy White told Bob in a postgame interview that surely Texas was good enough to be the national champion. OU's only consolation was that the Sooners held Texas to 272 yards, half the Longhorns' average for the first half of the season.

For Bob, it was the first of many trips to the Texas State Fair and the annual border battle in the Cotton Bowl. Bob had listened to many OU games on radio, but never imagined he would broadcast such a historical event to hundreds of thousands of OU fans back home in the Sooner State.

Bob was introduced to the OU-Texas game as a broadcaster during a period when Texas was dominating OU. In 1960, the Sooners were blanked 24-0. During this drought for OU, veteran columnist Ray Parr chided his readers in *The Daily Oklahoman* about spending hard-earned money to travel to Dallas to see OU get beat again:

Well, goodbye, chumps—all 25,000 of you—go on down there and beat your brains out. Let 'em push you around, trample you to death, gyp you out of your dough, ruin your health, and frazzle your nerves. You know you're not going to have a good time. You've tried it before. You'll come dragging back in here late Sunday, hating yourself, hating Texas, kicking your wife, and wondering how you are going to pay the grocery bill.[8]

Bob quickly discovered how serious OU fans were about beating Texas. The OU-Texas game was an even larger spectacle during the football season than the game against in-state rival Oklahoma State University (OSU). Coaches recruited with a sense of "How will this player help us beat Texas?" Dan Jenkins gave a time-worn colorful description of the OU-Texas game in *Sports Illustrated:*

If Yale vs. Harvard can best be described as an intellectual rivalry, the Texas-Oklahoma game is just the opposite. It is raw, rugged, and deadly serious. Fights frequently break out in the stands as well as on the field. It features some of the most aggressive tackling in the sport. At the moment of the kick off the players are jumping up and down, as if they've swallowed something from the chemistry lab, and waving their arms in the manner of John Wayne leading his troops in a charge out of the trenches. The bands are simultaneously

*bursting forth with "The Eyes of Texas" and "Boomer Sooner"
and more than 75,000 maniacs, pretty evenly divided, are
standing and screeching.*[9]

Even after losing to Texas, coached by former Sooner quarterback Darrell Royal, Wilkinson never lost confidence in his 1961 team, even though he privately said that it was the "low water mark of recent Oklahoma football."[10] Wilkinson told some Sooner players that OU would win its next five games. It was one thing to make that declaration privately, but Wilkinson completely went against his normal, calm demeanor and made the statement on his weekly television show. Co-host Howard Neumann was shocked after he asked Wilkinson how he saw the season. Wilkinson said, "I think we're going to win the next five."

Bob believed in Wilkinson's ability as a coach, but doubted if OU could beat Kansas State, Missouri, that was ranked in the top ten, Army, Nebraska, and OSU. The Sooners beat Kansas State and Missouri and headed for a national showdown with Army at Yankee Stadium in New York City. Bob already had been at Notre Dame Stadium earlier in the season, so going into another famous sports venue like Yankee Stadium was becoming "old hat."

Occasionally, Wilkinson used trick plays. Before the Army game, he told Bob of a particular trick play he might use "if the game depended upon it." Bob arrived at Yankee Stadium early and helped Bill Bryan set up the equipment necessary to tap into the telephone line to broadcast the action back to Oklahoma. In the open air press box were some of the nation's leading sportscasters and sportswriters, among them Howard Cosell.[11]

When Army was on defense, the players huddled far from the line of scrimmage and came up to the line slowly. Wilkinson designed a two-part trick play. The quarterback handed off to a half-back, who gained two or three yards, and went down. The Sooner player handed the ball to the referee and acted as if the OU team was returning to its huddle. However, there was no huddle, simply a quick return to the line, a fast count, and a lateral to Mike McClellan who ran for OU's first touchdown. OU won the game 14-8. The headline in the next morning's edition of the *New York Times* said, "Sooners outflank Army." [12]

Other sports reporters in the press box were impressed with how smoothly Bob reported the trick play. One New York writer, Red Smith, not knowing that Bob knew that the trick play would be called, said, "Son, I don't know who you are, but you called that play beautifully." Bob said, "Thank you!" [13]

After the game, Wilkinson, his assistant coach, Gomer Jones, and players greeted the media with incredible enthusiasm. Bob said, "You would have thought the Sooners had just won another national championship. It was more emotion than I had seen from Wilkinson all season."

Bob learned in a humorous way that his wife, Joan, and his brother's wife, Barbara, had passed up a chance to see the game at Yankee Stadium. They gave their tickets to two sailors they met on the street and spent the afternoon shopping. Bob and Jack, who had for a short time helped Bob with statistics at the game, were back in their hotel rooms when their wives arrived with their arms filled with "many boxes and sacks" from the shopping trip. [14]

Bob's friends, Lee Thompson, Jr., and his brother, Ralph, traveled to New York in an unusual way. They donned their old Air Force uniforms and boarded a military transport plane at Tinker Air Force Base for a flight to the New York City area. They knocked on Bob's hotel room door the night before the game and promptly saluted him.[15]

In the next two weeks, OU defeated Nebraska and OSU. Sportswriters around the country said that OU's comeback was the top sports story of the year and that it was Wilkinson's finest coaching job. The 1961 season was not a winning year for OU, but it also was not a second consecutive losing season. Wilkinson privately confided in Bob that he was very proud of the comeback effort, but reflected, "OU needs more players quickly." [16]

One history-making event occurred for the Sooners in 1961. The Bartlett family in Sapulpa, Oklahoma, donated the use of a Sooner Schooner for home games in Norman. Powered by two white Shetland ponies, named "Ike" and "Mike" after the popular candy, the schooner was reminiscent of wagons used by pioneers in the Oklahoma Land Run in 1889. The Sooner Schooner was not officially recognized as a Sooner mascot until 1980.

During his first year as play-by-play announcer for OU football, Bob developed a rigorous set of principles that has guided his career. He intentionally did not use sports slang expressions. He said, "I just wanted to tell the listener what was happening on the field, nothing but the facts." Bob wanted credibility with the audience. "Without trust of the listener, it would be a useless exercise in futility," he said. Bob believed his only job was to fairly and accurately describe the action and to keep the audience informed and entertained. He had excitement in his voice, but he nevertheless stuck to a straightforward description of every play and situation on the field before him. By the end of the season, Bob knew play-by-play was his "life's work" and all the other more mundane parts of a job in broadcasting from sales to newscasts and sportscasts were "simply necessary to make play-by-play work possible." [17]

After football season concluded, Bob began preparing to broadcast OU basketball games. There was no doubt that OU's emphasis in athletics was football. In fact, the OU Athletic Department could not interest any radio stations in Oklahoma City or Tulsa to air Sooner basketball games. Only KNOR in Norman and KWCO in Chickasha, Oklahoma, agreed to carry some of the OU basketball games in the 1961-1962 season. In previous years, OU basketball was not very popular and KNOR carried OSU games even though the station was in the hometown of OU.

Bob was not overly confident about his play-by-play ability in basketball. Admittedly, he had never played or watched basketball in high school and college. Bob said, "I knew nothing about the game. I didn't know the slang terms or expressions used by coaches and fans. I simply called the action on the court. I did not try to describe the form of defense being employed on a particular play because I didn't know what it was."

In fact, for his first year, Bob used the term "mechanical error" instead of "turnover." He had picked up the term from previous OU basketball play-by-play announcer L.H. Bengston, the voice of the basketball Sooners in the late 1950s. When a coach chided Bob for using the "ridiculous" words of "mechanical error," Bob stopped and began using the more modern term of "turnover." [18]

OU had moderate success on the basketball court from 1908 to 1961, with only a dozen losing records in the period. The Sooners made it to their first Final Four in 1939 and lost the national championship game to Holy Cross University in 1947.

When Bob began broadcasting OU basketball games, Doyle Parrack had been coach of the basketball Sooners since 1956. A native of Cotton County, Oklahoma, Parrack played on the 1945 Oklahoma A & M national championship team. After spending one season with the Chicago Stags of the National Basketball Association (NBA), he became an assistant coach at Oklahoma City University (OCU). When Coach Abe Lemons left OCU, Parrack became the Chiefs' head basketball coach. Even with a quality basketball coach such as Parrack, the Sooners hardly ever filled the 4,775-seat OU Fieldhouse on the Norman campus.

Bob did play-by-play for all home basketball games, but away games were aired only if they were of great interest. In the first few years, Bob broadcast less than half the away games each season. There were no expenses in the budget for Bob's travel. There was no doubt the OU Athletic Department saw basketball as just another sport in the shadow of OU football.

OU apparently was happy with Bob's play-by-play of the Sooners football campaign in 1961 and he was welcomed with open arms for the 1962 season. However, the color commentator job was awarded to Jack Ogle, much to Bob's delight.

"Jack had an incredible voice, had played sports, and knew how to analyze what was happening on the field," Bob remembered. Fans listening on the radio agreed that Bob and Jack had a special chemistry. Bob talked fast, Jack was more methodical. The contrast in styles was well received. Lee Allan Smith said, "Bob's sense of humor set him apart from other play-by-play announcers. He and Jack fed off each other and delighted audiences. Everyone wanted to listen to them." [19]

Bob and Jack Ogle, left, had a special chemistry as they teamed to broadcast OU and OSU football games for more than 20 years. Ogle's greatest legacy may be his three sons who have been prominent in the Oklahoma City television market for decades. Kevin and Kent are news anchors at KFOR-TV and Kelly is a news anchor at KWTV.

Bob won his first sportscasting award in 1962 when he was named Oklahoma Sportscaster of the Year in a poll conducted by the National Sportswriters and Sportscasters Association of Salisbury, North Carolina. It was the first of 15 such awards during Bob's career.[20]

Bob accompanied the Sooners to Dallas in early October, 1962, to play top-ranked Texas. Sooner fans believed this could be the year that the Sooners could break the Longhorns' domination. But OU came up short, losing to Texas 9-6. After the hard-fought game, Wilkinson said in the locker room, "I thought we played as good as we could. The Texas players knew they had been hit." [21]

Each year after the game with Texas, OU began its grueling Big Eight Conference schedule. The conference was made up of OU, Nebraska, Kansas, OSU, Kansas State, Iowa State, Colorado, and Missouri. The Sooners had competed in what was called the

Big Six Conference with Iowa State, Missouri, Nebraska, Kansas, and Kansas State from 1920 to 1948 when the addition of Colorado resulted in the formation of the Big Seven Conference. OSU joined the conference in 1958. From that date until its dissolution with the formation of the Big 12 Conference in 1996, the eight-team conference was known as the Big Eight.

OU played each of its seven conference opponents annually in Big Eight competition. Every other year, Bob visited every Big Eight venue in football and basketball. OU was lucky to have good facilities in Norman. However, that was not in case in several of the Big Eight towns.

In the early 1960s, Nebraska's press box in Lincoln was unofficially voted by sports information directors as the worst in the country. Bob and Jack had to climb a ladder to reach the shabbily-built radio press box. The four-story structure literally swayed in the wind. The actual broadcast booth was so small that only Bob and Ogle could fit inside. Their engineer had to stand in a nearby hallway.[22]

Several hours before the 1962 OU-Kansas game in Lawrence, Kansas, Bob and Ogle were getting ready to go to the stadium. Bob had just taken his clothes off to walk into the shower of the hotel room where he and Ogle were staying in downtown Lawrence. Suddenly, the room began swaying. Bob had no idea that earthquakes occurred in Kansas. A little frightened, Bob took a quick shower, dressed, and he and Ogle headed to the football stadium. There was another problem for the broadcast team caused by the earthquake. Bob and Jack got stuck in the elevator with *The Daily Oklahoman* sports reporter Bob Hurt on the way to the top of the stadium to the press box. Fortunately, they pounded on the door until they were rescued. Bob stood on his equipment suitcase to summon help.[23]

The 1962 season was the culmination of several years of rebuilding. Except for losses to Texas and Notre Dame, OU won the Big Eight Conference championship, despite the fact that only two starters returned from the year before. With stars such as Monte Deere and Leon Cross, the Sooners rose to No. 8 in the final Associated Press poll. As a reward for winning the Big Eight, OU was invited to play the University of Alabama in the Orange Bowl in Miami, Florida, on the first day of 1963.

Before the bowl game, Bob began another season of broadcasting OU basketball games. The Sooners' new men's basketball coach was Bob Stevens. In his first game in December, 1962, OU set an all-time scoring record with 96 points in a win over Southern Methodist University in Dallas. Stevens' new fast-break offense, called Bob Stevens' Go-Go Sooners, caused Bob to sit on the edge of his seat all night. He remembered, "There was no time for catching my breath while someone walked the ball up the floor. As soon as SMU scored or gave up the ball, the Sooners were headed back to the other goal at break-neck speed."[24]

It was a star-studded Orange Bowl game, both on the field and off on the first day of the new year. Before the game, President John F. Kennedy visited the OU locker room. Kennedy and Wilkinson were friends. The president had appointed Wilkinson as Special Consultant for Physical Fitness, a White House-level post intended to promote physical fitness among America's youth.

OU lost to Alabama 17-0, largely due to the quarterbacking of Joe Namath. Even though the Sooners lost the game, the season was successful. All-American Leon Cross, co-captain of the 1962 Sooner team, told Bob in the locker room after the game, "The season was great all because of Coach Wilkinson. He sets a good example for us. He taught us so much more than football. He taught us how to get along in the real world." [25]

Bob turned his attention to OU basketball. There still was no money to pay his travel expenses for out-of-town games, so he traveled on the team bus and roomed with Coach Stevens. Once, Bob had to borrow Stevens' razor. For many years when Stevens saw Bob, he asked, "You want to borrow my razor?" [26]

As spring football began in 1963, Wilkinson looked for answers for his struggling Sooners. For the first time in his coaching career, he recruited a junior college transfer. Joe Don Looney had spent two years at Cameron Junior College in Lawton, Oklahoma. He was an unknown, but did not remain so for long. In the opening game of the season, Looney ran for a 60-yard touchdown against Syracuse University and began working on his legend as a wonderful football player and "unmanageable revolutionary." [27]

Looney did not like the discipline required by Wilkinson at OU. During one practice, Looney asked Wilkinson why he had to practice if he knew all the plays and was in good shape. That did not go over well with the discipline-conscious Wilkinson. Wilkinson "dropped the hammer" on Looney after OU lost to Texas and senior football players voted to kick Looney off the team. [28]

Looney's dismissal from the team was no surprise or disappointment to Bob. Following one of the early season games, Bob attempted to interview Looney in the locker room. Looney nearly knocked the microphone out of Bob's hand and retorted, "I ain't got time for anything like this!" [29]

After Looney left the Sooners, OU won its next six games and prepared for the November 23 game against Nebraska. Tragically, President Kennedy was assassinated in Dallas, Texas, on November 22. Many college games were canceled, but Wilkinson spoke to Robert Kennedy, the president's brother, who encouraged him to play the game.

The nation was stunned by Kennedy's assassination. Bob, Jack, the broadcast crew, and Sooner coaches and players found it difficult to concentrate on the game. They wished they were home with their families in this time of national tragedy. Nebraska won the game 29-20.

Ralph Thompson, later a member of the Oklahoma legislature, an esteemed and nationally well-respected federal judge, was in the press box working as a spotter for Bob. The stadium at Nebraska was silent as the teams came on the field. Thompson remembered:

It was awkward and tense for everyone. No one wanted to seem disrespectful. No one knew exactly what to do. But Bob's natural, instinctive good nature and good will allowed him to call a great game. He did it in a way that let us in the broadcast booth and all the listeners back home enjoy the game without feeling disrespectful toward the slain President or to the tragic event. He was just being Bob. I will never forget it.[30]

The broadcast "was quite unusual," Bob said. The network decided to eliminate commercials and instead play soft, funeral music during commercial breaks. Local stations were advised they had the option of playing the music or inserting local commercials.

OU closed out the 1963 season with a win over OSU. It was Wilkinson's last game. Earlier in the year, he had decided to run for the United States Senate from Oklahoma. Even though Oklahoma was traditionally a Democratic state, Wilkinson's advisers told him he was the most popular person in the state, and, if he changed his registration to Republican, he could defeat Democratic Senator J. Howard Edmondson who had been appointed to the position when Senator Robert S. Kerr died on January 1, 1963.

Bob broke the story of Wilkinson resigning to run for the Senate seat, but got the scoop in an unusual way. Bob was still on the air at KNOR from 6:15 a.m. to 10:00 a.m. each morning and received a call from his friend Dick Reynolds of Reynolds Ford. Reynolds happened to be driving by the Cleveland County courthouse in Norman and saw Wilkinson walking in the door of the courthouse where the County Election Board was located. That meant only one thing to Bob—Wilkinson was changing his registration. Later that morning, Bob reported the event on the air. Wilkinson soon confirmed the report. He later asked Bob, "How did you know what I was doing?" [31]

In the next year's election, Edmondson was upset by Democratic State Senator Fred Harris of Lawton in the Democratic primary. Even though Wilkinson was a popular Republican nominee, he was defeated by Harris in the general election in November, 1964. Part of the problem for Wilkinson was that President Lyndon B. Johnson carried Oklahoma heavily over Republican presidential hopeful Barry Goldwater.

Wilkinson's career at OU was superb. In 17 seasons, he made the Split-T offense famous and won three national championships and 14 conference championships. He won 82 percent of his games and finished his collegiate career with a record of 145-29-4. He later joined ABC Sports and was the color commentator on ABC's college game of the week with play-by-play announcers Chris

Schenkel and Keith Jackson. Wilkinson coached the NFL St. Louis Cardinals in 1978 and 1979. He was inducted into the College Football Hall of Fame before his death in 1994.[32]

Bob was sad to see Wilkinson leave the Sooners head-coaching job. Even though he was never close friends with Wilkinson, the coach obviously respected his talent in the broadcast booth. On one occasion, Wilkinson invited Bob to his home with some of the nation's top sportswriters. Bob also was present at weekly visits the coach had with students at Oklahoma Memorial Union.[33]

Wilkinson played a major role in choosing his assistant, Gomer Jones, as his successor as head football coach. Bob had a closer relationship with Jones than with Wilkinson.

Jones had been one of the outstanding collegiate football players of the 1930s. He was the anchor of the Ohio State University offensive line, team captain, and the leading tackler from his linebacker position on defense. Later inducted into the College Football Hall of Fame, Jones was a consensus All-American in 1935 and was drafted by the Chicago Cardinals of the National Football League. However, he passed up a professional playing career to pursue coaching.

Jones was an assistant coach at Ohio State until he joined Wilkinson's staff at OU. He was a loyal and faithful top assistant to Wilkinson for 17 years, developed 16 All-American linemen, and was the architect of Oklahoma's great lines during the championship seasons in the 1950s.

Unfortunately, the OU coaching staff had not done a great job of recruiting new players in the early 1960s. Bob explained, "For years, good players from Oklahoma, Texas, and the region wanted to come to Oklahoma—they didn't have to be recruited. As other programs grew stronger and OU faltered, the lack of consistent recruiting became a crisis." Another problem was that the OU coaching staff was primarily made up of former players who had no previous coaching experience.[34]

"Gomer was one of the guys," Bob said. Jones and SID Keith gave Bob sufficient time to find out the status of Sooner player injuries and figuring out depth charts. Pre-game interviews were not part of the broadcast, but Bob used information he gleaned from meetings with Jones and Keith to provide fans the latest information about OU.[35]

Jones' tenure as head coach began poorly. After beating Maryland, the Sooners lost three straight games, gave up 40 points to the University of Southern California, and were thrashed by Texas. Finishing the 1964 season at 6-3-1, the Sooners were invited to play Florida State University in the Gator Bowl. Early on the morning of the game, Bob learned from Keith that four players were dismissed from the squad for prematurely signing professional football contracts. The players, halfbacks Lance Rentzel and Wes Skidgel, fullback Jim Grisham, and All-American tackle Ralph Neely, were sorely missed as OU lost the bowl game 36-19.[36]

For two seasons Jones led the Sooners as head coach. There was little success and Bob could see that Jones was not enjoying himself holding down two roles, as athletic director and head football coach. After losses, players blamed other players for failure— there was no doubt there was dissension on the team.

The frustration with Jones' performance as head coach of the Sooners almost cost Jack Ogle his job as color commentator in 1965. After students had burned Jones in effigy at a bonfire the night before a home game, Ogle led off his part of the pre-game show the next week at Pittsburgh by saying, "This is a do or die game for Gomer Jones." OU Athletic Director Ken Farris was livid and wanted Ogle fired. Even Coach Jones' wife was quite vocal. However, Bob went to bat for Ogle. After all, some of the people who publicly were upset with Ogle's comments were actually thinking the same thing.[37]

The 1965 season was worse than the year before. OU finished 3-7 and supporters demanded a new coach. Bob was friends with several members of The Touchdown Club whose membership included some of OU's largest supporters and state business leaders. University President George L. Cross was approached by Touchdown Club President Bob Bowers and Eugene Jordan. In 1998, at age 93, Cross remembered the meeting as the conveyance of a threat that OU's top money supporters would withdraw their support of the athletic department unless Jones was gone.[38]

Cross said he would not remove Jones, and suggested to Bowers and Jordan that they communicate their feelings directly to the coach. Several Touchdown Club members privately told Jones that OU football needed to go in a different direction. After several weeks, Jones resigned, but remained as athletic director.[39]

The search for a new football coach began feverishly. Many OU fans wanted to lure Darrell Royal from the University of Texas where he had become a successful head coach. However, OU could not meet the financial package Royal enjoyed at Texas.

In December, 1965, the OU Board of Regents hired University of Arkansas assistant coach Jim Mackenzie as OU's 15th football coach. An OU fan gave Bob a "Welcome Coach Mackenzie" bumper sticker that he promptly applied to the rear bumper of his automobile.[40]

Mackenzie had played college football at the University of Kentucky and had been on the Kentucky squad that beat OU in the 1951 Sugar Bowl. Bob had attended that game in New Orleans with his brother, Jack.

Bob found Mackenzie to be friendly, knowledgeable about football, and accessible to the press and fans alike. Mackenzie cleaned house and hired all new assistant coaches. Bob remembered, "There was a great feeling in Norman among OU supporters that this was a new day and OU could return to the glory days of Wilkinson." [41]

Bob and Joan, back row, with Frank, left front, and Bobby at a Christmas party at the home of Earl Sneed in Norman in 1965.

One of the first things Mackenzie did was to change the color of OU football helmets from white to red. Mackenzie was accustomed to red helmets at Arkansas and thought the change was right for OU, although some Sooner fans objected at first.

The Barrys moved into a new home in 1965, a two-story house at 1809 Thorton Drive just north of Main Street in Norman's Westwood Estates subdivision. There were few homes on the land surrounding the house. On the day Frank and Bobby were taken to the new house by their parents, Bobby, trying to remove a "for sale" sign, broke a front window. "I got in trouble right off the bat," he said.[42] The Barrys lived just two blocks from Coach Mackenzie and his family.

Bob spent a lot of time in the spring of 1966 getting to know the new football coaching staff. Chuck Fairbanks was the defensive backfield coach. Homer Rice was the offensive coordinator, Pat James was the defensive coordinator, and Barry Switzer, an assistant to Frank Broyles for six years at Arkansas, was the offensive line coach.

In addition to spending more time than usual preparing for a football season at OU, Bob had other things on his mind. His friend and color commentator on OU football broadcasts, Jack Ogle, was encouraging him to make a career move—at least part time—to television.

CHAPTER FIVE

Television Anchor

From the first night Bob did sports news on television, the audience loved him. They could tell he knew his business and communicated scores and highlights in a straightforward and respectful manner.

—LEE ALLAN SMITH

Bob loved radio. He had been in the radio business at KNOR for a decade, both on the air and as an advertising salesman and sales manager. However, his prominence as voice of the OU football and basketball teams put him in frequent contact with other radio, television, and print journalists covering OU sports. Jack Ogle constantly tried to get Bob to consider moving to television. For the first four years of their friendship, Bob shrugged off any chance of him giving up his KNOR position for a television sportscasting job.

However, an opportunity "to ease into television" came in 1966 when Ogle told Bob that management at WKY-TV in Oklahoma City wanted a "fresh sports face." Ogle told Bob the job was his— all he had to do was commit to anchor the Sunday night sportscast on WKY-TV except for weekends when he was out of state broadcasting OU football or basketball games. The official offer of the position came from Lee Allan Smith in a telephone call.[1]

Joan agreed with Bob that television sports was becoming big business and that his future as a sports announcer might be best served by the weekend job in television. After all, if Bob did not like television, he still had his full-time job at KNOR.

WKY-TV was Oklahoma's oldest and most-watched television station. It began broadcasting on June 6, 1949, and was owned by the Oklahoma Publishing Company (OPUBCO), publisher of *The Daily Oklahoman*. The original studios were in the Oklahoma City Municipal Auditorium but had moved to new facilities on Britton Road in far north Oklahoma City. The station was the first television station in the United States to establish a meteorology department and the first non-network-owned station to broadcast local programs in color.[2]

WKY-TV's sister radio station was WKY-Radio, also owned by OPUBCO. WKY-Radio was the first radio station licensed by the Federal Communications Commission west of the Mississippi River. The station went on the air in 1922 in the living room and garage of the home of its founder, Earl Hull. Radio was a novelty and Hull only made enough from the sale of radio receivers to broadcast a few hours per week. When Hull began broadcasting, there were less than 30 radio receivers in Oklahoma City. OPUBCO bought WKY-Radio in 1928 for $5,000 and affiliated with the NBC Radio Network.[3]

The WKY family had more than its share of broadcasters who moved on to national broadcasting jobs. In addition to Walter Cronkite of CBS News, NBC's "The Today Show" host Frank McGee and variety television host Mike Douglas also had worked for either WKY-Radio or WKY-TV.

Bob interviewed with WKY-TV news director Ernie Schultz;

sports director, Ross Porter, who Bob had beat out in the OU football audition; and the station's assistant general manager, Lee Allan Smith. They agreed upon financial consideration and Bob began doing the Sunday night sportscast. Audiences were pleased. For five seasons OU fans had become accustomed to Bob's voice on OU football and basketball broadcasts.

In 1966, Bob began as the weekend sports anchor at WKY-TV. He worked with Mike Treps, right, who soon became Channel Four sports director following the departure of Ross Porter. The one desk was the entire space allocated to sports in the Channel Four newsroom.

When Bob went to work for WKY-TV, Ross Porter, left, was sports director. In 1966, his bosses at Channel Four, Lee Allan Smith, center, and Norman Bagwell, hosted a going-away party for Porter who moved to Los Angeles and became the voice of the Los Angeles Dodgers. *Courtesy Lee Allan Smith.*

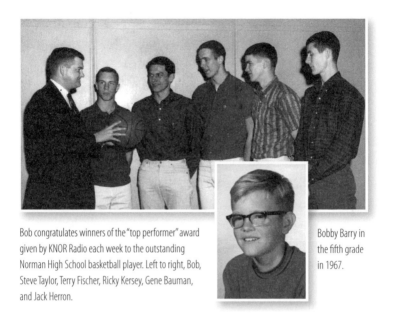

Bob congratulates winners of the "top performer" award given by KNOR Radio each week to the outstanding Norman High School basketball player. Left to right, Bob, Steve Taylor, Terry Fischer, Ricky Kersey, Gene Bauman, and Jack Herron.

Bobby Barry in the fifth grade in 1967.

Bob enjoyed working Sunday nights and appearing on the 10:00 p.m. 30-minute news, weather, and sports show with news anchors George Tomek and Charles Hoff and meteorologists Jim Williams and Herb Kershaw. The weeknight news anchor was Jack Ogle with Mike Treps doing sports and Jim Williams handling the primetime weather segments. Treps had replaced Ross Porter who moved to KABC Radio in Los Angeles, California. Lee Allan Smith had hired Treps, a graduate of OU, because of his local connections over Verne Lundquist, a Texas sportscaster who tried out for the job as WKY-TV sports director. Lundquist later became the voice of the Dallas Cowboys and one of the nation's premier television sports-casters for ABC-TV and CBS-TV.[4]

Williams had worked for the Gaylord broadcasting companies since 1958 when he moved to Oklahoma City from Muskogee. He got the job at Channel Four because his friend, Don Ferrell, later a prominent newspaper publisher, state senator, and Oklahoma's adjutant general, was the personnel director for the Oklahoma Publishing Company, part of the Gaylord empire.[5]

Williams enjoyed working with Bob on Sunday night news broadcasts. "I recognized immediately he was a real people person," Williams remembered, "He was a great communicator and everyone, from the cameramen to the anchors, loved him." Williams and his wife, Darlene, became good friends with Bob and Joan.[6]

Bob knew WKY-TV was an excellent proving ground in broadcasting. Even though he and news director Schultz had only a cordial relationship, Schultz respected Bob's abilities as a sports expert. Schultz, as news director, followed in the footsteps of Dick John and other anchors who had won the hearts of viewers in central Oklahoma for years. It was not unusual for Channel Four personalities to land jobs at the network level or in top ten markets. An example is Bob Dotson, who began as a news reporter for WKY-TV in 1969. He later began a stellar career as an investigative reporter and Emmy Award-winning journalist.

In addition to learning the television sports business, there were frequent celebrity sightings around WKY-TV on weekends. The station was the originating studio for country music singer Buck Owens' syndicated program, "The Buck Owens Ranch Show." It was not uncommon to see leading country music stars pull up in the "guest" parking slots behind the television station. The Buck Owens show was packaged by two Oklahoma City businessmen, Bud and Don Mathis, the original Mathis brothers. Also, WKY-Radio disc jockey Ronnie Kaye began hosting a popular weekly dance and music show, "The Scene."

New football coach Mackenzie's first season at OU in 1966 was a success. OU returned offensive starters Ron Shotts, Ben Hart, and Stanley Crowder. On defense, veteran middle guard Granville Liggins anchored the line that included Jim Riley and John Koller. An impressive group of sophomores took the field for the Sooners, including Bobby Warmack, Eddie Hinton, Gary Harper, and kicker, Mike Vachon.[7]

The highlight of the Sooner season came early in October when Oklahoma mascot, Kirke Kickingbird, "Little Red," led the team into the Cotton Bowl for the annual Red River Rivalry. Texas committed five turnovers and OU quarterback Warmack dominated the game, rushing for nearly 100 yards and completed 12 passes. Split end Ben Hart caught four of those passes. Warmack scored OU's only touchdown in an 18-9 victory.[8]

Oklahoma fans went crazy. Frank Boggs wrote in *The Daily Oklahoman:*

Those were Oklahomans out there challenging a steel goal post at the finish. Those were red and white pennants being waved wildly at the finish rather than being sat upon. Sooner players, with considerable help from delirious followers, hoisted coach Jim Mackenzie on their shoulders and paraded him toward the locker room. Assistants Galen Hall and Barry Switzer were given rides, too.[9]

From his post in the press box, Bob heard the Sooner fans that would not leave the stadium chanting, "We've won! We've Won!" and "Poor Texas, Poor Texas!" Police gave up trying to guard the goal posts that were quickly dismantled by OU fans. In the locker room, Texas coach Darrell Royal told Mackenzie, "Congratulations to you, Jim. That was a well-earned win." [10]

Bob, personally, was elated with the Sooner victory over the Longhorns, the first in the six years he had been broadcasting OU games. He said, "For awhile I thought we would never beat Texas again." [11]

OU's fortunes turned around from the previous season even though the Sooners finished 1966 with a 6-4 record. One of the losses was to eventual national champion Notre Dame. Another defeat was a one-point loss to OSU, for the second consecutive year. Despite the last-game loss, OU fans were extremely confident that new coach Mackenzie was on the right track.

Even though Bob had become a television sports anchor, he still did daily sports reports on KNOR Radio in the late 1960s.

Bob continued his job as sales manager at KNOR. To compensate for being away from the family on Sunday nights at WKY-TV, he tried to arrive home early Monday through Friday. To take some of the sales load from him, KNOR owner Bill Morgan hired OU college students such as Phil Caudill, Rick Parrish, Sandy Mc-Mahan, and Bob Burke to help Barry make weekly contact with advertisers, sell as many "spots" as possible, pick up copy for commercials, and record them in the KNOR production room. Bob still actively managed the affairs of the station but allowed other disc jockeys at KNOR to replace him on the air in the mornings, although Bob did ten-minute sports reports several times during the broadcast day. Morgan also was busy outside the station. He was elected mayor of Norman in 1967.

Bob continued to broadcast Norman High School football and basketball games live on KNOR. Such broadcasts involved coordinating the installation of a Class C telephone line in football stadium press boxes or making certain a line was available at the top of bleachers in high school gymnasiums that did not have formal press facilities. Bob and his color commentator, such as Burke in 1967 and 1968, often broadcast basketball games surrounded by fans. Bob held his starting lineups and other information on his knees and did the play-by-play while Burke kept statistics and read commercials live during timeouts. Fans sometimes harassed them during the game.[12]

It was always an incredible learning experience for young OU broadcasting students to travel with and work alongside Bob, who continued to perennially win the Sportscaster of the Year Award in Oklahoma. At the time, Burke was 18 and Bob was 36, twice Burke's age. Burke nicknamed Bob "Old Guard."

There was nothing luxurious about Bob and his crew traveling to towns such as Duncan to broadcast Norman High School sporting events. It meant Bob driving with his color man in his white Volkswagen beetle to some favorite restaurant in a town two hours before the game, quickly eating, then arriving at the stadium or gymnasium to test the telephone line before it was time to go on the air. Bob had been doing high school sports for a decade and knew the radio sportscasting business so well that the rigorous schedule really did not bother him. There was no stress involved, just methodically getting to the right town at the right time and doing his favorite thing in the world outside his family—talking about sports on radio.[13]

Broadcasting Norman High School home football games was quite an experience for Bob and his crew. The lighting for night games at OU's Owen Field in the 1960s was atrocious. Norman had black and orange uniforms. Bob remembered, "If there was any rain, the numbers became so covered in dirt and mud by the end of the first quarter, I had no idea who was running with the ball or who had made a tackle. It was a nightmare for whoever was spotting for me."[14]

At one NFL pre-season game played at Owen Field, a player for the Cleveland Browns walked out onto the field in the dimly-lit stadium and reportedly asked an OU official, "When will the lights be turned on?" The OU person said, "They are on, sir!"

Not all radio broadcasts were perfect. Once, Bob was calling a high school football game between Norman and Ardmore when he saw an official pick up the ball after a punt and begin walking down the field. Bob thought it was a penalty and said, "Well, an official is starting to walk off the penalty. There he goes, five, 10, 15, 20, 25, 30." About that time, the color commentator spoke up and said, "Bob, it's the end of the quarter. The referee is just going to the other end of the field." Bob had nothing further to say about the incident.[15]

In addition to sporting events, Bob also anchored other special broadcasts for KNOR. On election nights, City National Bank sponsored a live broadcast to report voting results. Don Symcox was in charge of advertising for the bank and invited Bob to host the election night remote from the lobby of the bank. The "City National

Election Central" consisted of a single telephone to obtain results from the election board and four adding machines.[16]

During football season, Symcox, clothing store owner Tom McCall, and insurance agent John Ford joined Bob on KNOR for a college game prediction show in which the four friends sat around the microphone guessing what team would prevail in the coming weekend's action.

The Symcox and Barry families became close. Mary Louise Symcox and Joan were members of a ladies bridge club. The families were so close that once the ladies overheard their sons playing and Bobby Barry calling Lee Symcox "Lee Barry." [17]

On April 29, 1967, Bob received a frantic telephone call from OU SID Harold Keith. The tragic news was that Coach Mackenzie had died the night before of a sudden heart attack at age 37, leaving a wife and two small children. Bob, thinking first of the heavy loss that Mackenzie's family must be feeling, began to spread the sad news among friends. Just the week before, Bob had talked to Mackenzie about spring practice and the possibilities for further improvement of the OU program for the 1967 season.[18]

Many prominent OU supporters wanted to take plenty of time to make a nationwide search for a new coach. However, OU President Cross believed a new coach and a new system coming so late in the year would be detrimental for the Sooners. He used his emergency powers and named assistant coach Chuck Fairbanks to succeed Mackenzie, subject to approval at the next meeting of the OU Board of Regents.[19]

Fairbanks, a graduate of Michigan State University, was only 33 years old. He had coached at Arizona State University and the University of Houston before joining Mackenzie's staff at OU in

1966. Bob already had a good working relationship with Fairbanks as an assistant coach, so his promotion to head coach made an easy transition for Bob as he prepared for a new football season.

However, Fairbanks was difficult to get to know well. "He had a cold exterior," Bob remembered, "but he knew football inside and out." Bob does not believe Fairbanks ever received due credit for building a foundation for greatness in the football program at OU.[20]

Fairbanks proved to be a great coach for OU. In six seasons, he won three Big Eight Conference titles and had two 11-1 seasons. In late 1972, he became coach of the NFL New England Patriots, making way for Barry Switzer to begin his era as OU's football coach. Fairbanks also later coached at the University of Colorado and in the United States Football League before retiring and establishing an automobile dealership in a suburb of Dallas.

Fairbanks' first OU team in 1967 suffered from heavy graduation losses on both the offensive and defensive lines, but returned quarterback Warmack, tailback Ron Shotts, fullback Gary Harper, and wingback Eddie Hinton who had led the nation in punt return yardage the previous season.

The Sooners barely lost to Texas, 9-7, a game that turned out to be the only loss of the season, but new faces began to appear for OU. Sophomore Steve Owens from Miami, Oklahoma, began to slash through holes in the line. He finished the season as the Big Eight Conference scoring and rushing leader. The Sooners beat all seven conference opponents, with only three games even close. Ranked No. 3 in both the Associated Press (AP) and United Press International (UPI) polls, OU was invited to the Orange Bowl to play the University of Tennessee. OU beat the Volunteers 26-24 and, with its 10-1 record, finished second in the nation. Granville

Liggins was a unanimous All-American selection at nose guard.[21]

Meanwhile, as basketball season began in earnest after the Christmas break, OU was showing off its new 29-year-old head coach, John MacLeod. After the previous season, five-year head coach Stevens resigned and the freshman coach, MacLeod, was named as his replacement.

Sportswriter Frank Boggs asked the question "Sooner Decision Too Hasty?" in his column in *The Daily Oklahoman*. Boggs' point was that OU seemed to be giving up any chance of excellence in the basketball program by naming MacLeod. After all, OU had lost at least ten games for a dozen seasons and had not won a conference championship since OU was a member of the Big Six Conference. Boggs kidded OU officials about "expanding the search for a coach" only from Lindsey Street to Main Street in Norman, rather than looking at coaches in other parts of the country.[22]

MacLeod quickly answered Boggs' concern by putting an exciting fast-break team onto the court in crimson-and-cream

uniforms. Bob liked MacLeod's businesslike approach and his emphasis on strong defense. In his first pre-game show with Bob, MacLeod expressed confidence that his players would work hard and become winners.

Frank Barry, left, and Bobby Barry, were active teenagers in junior high school in the late 1960s.

When Bob asked MacLeod what his slogan might be, the coach said, "Just win." [23]

MacLeod was a handsome young coach who traveled extensively around the state to promote OU basketball that had taken a distant back seat to OU football. The interest generated by the new Sooner coach caused several more radio stations to want to carry OU basketball games. The Sooner Basketball Network expanded to a half dozen stations and Bob hired OU Fieldhouse public address announcer and KNOR announcer Bob Burke as the first color commentator on the newly-expanded basketball network of stations. Burke was paid $25 per game. In previous years, Bob had broadcast Sooner basketball games by himself.

Bob became close friends with MacLeod and Denny Price, a former Norman High School and OU star basketball player, hired by MacLeod as an assistant coach. The three friends often spent time in the summer together talking about basketball and playing golf. Price, who played professional basketball for the Phillips 66ers, later was head basketball coach at Phillips University in Enid, Oklahoma, and taught the game to his three young sons, who were ages five, three, and six months when their father joined MacLeod's staff. Mark Price later was a two-time American point guard at Georgia Tech University and played 12 seasons in the NBA. He is the NBA's all-time leader in free throw shooting percentage. Matt Price played college basketball at Phillips University. The youngest Price son, Brent, was a basketball star at OU in the early 1990s before playing 11 years in the NBA.

During the basketball season, Bob spent a lot of time in hotels on the road in the Big Eight Conference towns. It was customary for OU to play Saturday in one town and Monday in another conference town. Bob stayed with the team for the Saturday to Monday trips. Coach MacLeod was a strict disciplinarian, he would not allow players to wear caps or hats indoors, and made them go to church on Sunday mornings.

Bob, right, and former OU quarterback Bobby Warmack compare notes before a spring football game.

Garfield Heard starred for the Sooners in 1969-1970 to lead OU to the National Invitation Tournament and end a 22-year post-season drought. *Courtesy University of Oklahoma Athletic Department.*

In Bob's estimation, there was no doubt MacLeod improved the Sooner basketball program. He stayed six seasons and took the Sooners to the National Invitation Tournament (NIT) in 1970 and 1971. Before 1970, the Sooner basketball squad had not appeared in a post-season tournament since 1947. After his stint at OU, MacLeod coached three different National Basketball Association teams, the Phoenix Suns, Dallas Mavericks, and New York Knicks. He also coached University of Notre Dame men's basketball for eight seasons.

There were some rough times during MacLeod's tenure at OU. During a game between OU and Texas A & M at the old field house, African American OU students were upset that the Aggies had no African American starters while four of OU's starters were African American. The protest after the game grew heated and Coach MacLeod had to leave the arena under police escort.[24]

In September, 1968, Bob joined other WKY reporters and personalities Danny Williams, Jack Ogle, and Mike Treps in broadcasting hourly reports on radio and twice-daily reports on television from the PGA Team Championship. The PGA played at Quail Creek Country Club and Twin Hills Country Club in Oklahoma City.

Bob "really liked" getting to hang out with some of the nation's best golfers at the tournament that was won by Bobby Nichols and George Archer. Bob and the golfers fought a light mist and gusty winds on the first day of the tournament. Professional golfers interviewed by Bob during the tournament included Tom Weiskopf, Tommy Aaron, Don January, Miller Barber, Hale Irwin, Jack Nicklaus, and Arnold Palmer. The latter two golfing legends played together as a team and finished far back from the leaders.[25]

Fairbanks lost again to Texas in 1968, a heart-breaking, hard-fought 28-20 loss. After the game, when he was told that Texas coach Royal said it was the most exciting of the 16 OU-Texas games in which he had played or coached, Fairbanks said, "I agree it was an exciting game, but I'd rather have won it and it be dull." [26]

OU averaged 35 points per game for the remainder of the season, losing only to Colorado, and tying Kansas for the Big Eight title. Steve Owens again led the Big Eight in rushing. The Sooners finished No. 10 in the final UPI poll and lost to Southern Methodist University in the Astro-Bluebonnet Bowl in Houston, Texas.[27]

Running back Steve Owens from Miami, Oklahoma, won the Heisman Trophy in 1969, the first Sooner to win the award since Billy Vessels in 1952. Owens later became athletic director at OU. *Courtesy University of Oklahoma Athletic Department.*

In Bob's first eight seasons as the voice of the Sooners, he worked with four different head coaches, a dozen assistant coaches, and hundreds of players. But none of the players impressed him more than running back Steve Owens who saved his best season for his senior campaign.

In 1969, Owens rushed for 1,523 yards and 23 touchdowns. He holds the top seven spots in the record book for most carries in a game. He set the record of 55 rushing attempts in his final game, a one-point win over OSU. Owens became the second OU Sooner to win the Heisman Trophy. He later played six seasons in the NFL with the Detroit Lions, was inducted into the College Football Hall of Fame, and served as OU's athletic director in the 1990s.

In 1969, Owens was surrounded by a cast of players whose names are high in Sooner lore. Ken Mendenhall was an All-American and a team captain along with Owens, Jim Files, and All-American Steve Zabel. Mendenhall played 11 seasons in the NFL and Zabel, one of OU's most versatile players ever, as a punter and receiver, was named to the All-American team and played for three teams in the NFL. Zabel and Bob became good friends.

Another of Bob's favorite players on the 1969 team was quarterback Jack Mildren, a sophomore. Mildren passed the ball with great efficiency. By his senior year, Mildren won All-American honors and was drafted in the second round by the Baltimore Colts. He served as lieutenant governor of Oklahoma from 1991 to 1995.

In spring practice in 1970, Bob spent a lot of time observing members of an incredible recruiting class that Fairbanks and his assistant coaches had put together. Sixteen of the players were from the State of Texas, two of whom would become two-time consensus All-Americans—halfback Greg Pruitt and center Tom Brahaney— and two more one-time All Americans—tackles Eddie Foster and Derland Moore.

Bob and Lee Allan Smith, Bob's high school friend, mentor, and boss at WKY-TV.

Bob and Joan, center, are congratulated on his selection as Oklahoma Sportscaster of the Year at a banquet sponsored by the National Association of Sportswriters and Sportscasters in Salisbury, North Carolina.

When Bob became sports director at WKY-TV, he joined Oklahoma City's top-rated television broadcast news team. Left to right, Bob, news anchor Jack Ogle, weatherman Jim Williams, and news anchor George Tomek.

In September, 1970, Bob faced another career decision. It was no secret that WKY-TV's general manager, Lee Allan Smith, wanted to replace sports director Mike Treps. While Treps was in Cincinnati, Ohio, doing a story on Oklahoma major league baseball star Johnny Bench, Smith called Bob to his office and offered him the job as full-time sports director. Bob did not ask any questions and assumed that Treps had taken another job.[28]

As soon as Bob arrived home that night, he and Joan had a long talk about their future. The multiple roles of working both at KNOR and WKY-TV, and his September to March assignment of football and basketball broadcasts each year, was beginning to weigh heavily upon Bob who was nearing the age of 40. Joan was completely supportive of whatever decision Bob made. He had enjoyed showing up on Sundays at the television station and putting together a sportscast. But he realized that being the sports director would entail much more—he would be in charge of the entire sports department and have personnel and coverage decisions to make. He told Joan, "If I fail as an on-the-air talent, I can always sell—everybody needs sales people." [29]

Together Bob and Joan decided, "Let's try it." Within the next few days, Bob learned Treps was given a job as community relations director and was scheduled to do weekend sports. The way in which Bob replaced him strained their relationship forever, even in decades later when they broadcast football games together. Bob said, "It was clumsy. I had worked for him—now he worked for me. He knew I didn't have anything to do with him losing the sports director's job, but he understandably resented management." [30]

Bob resigned his job at KNOR and became the full-time sports anchor at Channel Four, joining Jack Ogle and Jim Williams in primetime 30-minute weeknight news shows at 6:00 p.m. and 10:00 p.m.

Texas still had OU's number in the Cotton Bowl matchup in October, 1970. The Longhorns won 41-9. Texas had prevailed for the fourth straight year and for the 12th time in the previous 13 years. As he walked off the field, assistant coach Barry Switzer

For decades, the Barrys' frequent travel companions were Don and Mary Louise Symcox of Norman. Left to right, Don Symcox, Mary Louise Symcox, Joan Barry, and Bob.

looked up at the scoreboard and swore to himself he would never be beaten like that again, "no matter what it took." [31]

The only good thing for OU football that came out of the game was the unveiling of the Wishbone offense, a phenomenon that would become heavenly to OU fans during the next decade. Bob and Jack Ogle did not know the Wishbone would be unveiled in that game, although it was apparent that the Veer formation was not going to work for OU. In the pre-game warmup, Bob looked down to the floor of the Cotton Bowl and saw a number 30. He asked Ogle, "Who is number 30?" On closer examination, he discovered it was former wide receiver Greg Pruitt who had been given a new jersey number but still had number 83 on his helmet. That was a major clue to Bob and Ogle that the new formation was about to appear. [32]

At first, Bob did not know what to call the new formation. Until the name, "Wishbone," stuck, Bob called it the "Y" formation.

On that day, however, the Wishbone still had lots of kinks and quarterback Mildren and his running backs were bruised and battered in the locker room. Mildren told Bob in a post-game interview, "I was loving the new offense for awhile, but we made too many mistakes." [33]

Columnist Frank Boggs wrote about the devastating loss in the Sunday newspaper:

Anyone who thinks capital punishment has ended should have witnessed this one. By the time the long awaited fourth quarter began when OU fans traditionally wave four fingers at the team reminding them that the fourth quarter "belongs" to Oklahoma, most of our red-clad Sooner fans among the Cotton Bowl mob had left for the state fair midway, probably in hopes they'd be hurled off some ride. [34]

Even with sportswriters on his back for going to the Wishbone offense, Fairbanks proved them wrong in successive weeks of the 1970 season. The Sooners rushed for 519 yards in a 66-6 rout of OSU. With a 7-4 record, OU faced Coach Bear Bryant's Alabama team in the Astro-Bluebonnet Bowl in Houston. Greg Pruitt scored on runs of 58 and 25 yards in an exciting 24-24 standoff.

One of the perks of being sports director at WKY-TV was making all-expense paid trips to cover major sporting events. Bob traveled to Miami, Florida, for Super Bowl V in January, 1971, between the Dallas Cowboys and Baltimore Colts. Behind the arm of quarterback Johnny Unitas, the Colts beat Dallas 16-13 on a last-second field goal.

During the long career of Abe Lemons, right, as men's basketball coach at Oklahoma City University, Bob hosted Lemons' weekly coaches show on WKY-TV. The show was simply called "Abe."

In preparation for Super Bowl V, Bob flew to Miami with WKY-TV news reporter Bob Dotson. Management wanted a special produced on the big game. Bob and Dotson named the special program "The Long and Winding Road." Dotson rented a helicopter and flew over the Orange Bowl for aerial shots.

During the flight to Miami, Bob gave Dotson a piece of advice he never forgot. In a casual conversation with the 24-year-old journalist, Bob said, "The only way you will ever survive this business is to make yourself one of a kind, not one of many. You may not be one of a kind, but just the idea of it will keep you alert enough to do good work." [35]

In a pre-game interview Bob was embarrassed when he was talking on camera with Colts' receiver John Mackie. Back in Oklahoma, Bob was friends with Wayne Mackie, a reporter for *The Daily Oklahoman*. During the interview with "John" Mackie, Bob called him "Wayne." Startled, Mackie said, "Wayne, where did you get Wayne?" Bob tried to explain that he knew Wayne Mackie in Oklahoma. John Mackie was not amused. [36]

When Bob was interviewing Dallas coach Tom Landry, Dotson said, "Bob, hang on a minute!" Dotson opened the camera and out fell 200-feet of film. Coach Landry looked at Bob and Dotson and said, "I'll come back later." [37]

To make matters worse, there was not enough room in the Orange Bowl press box for Bob, so stadium officials put him and other reporters in the stands. Bob caught a terrible cold and coughed much of the game. The final blow came when he returned home and WKY-TV decided to run the 60-minute special at 11:00 a.m. on Sunday morning. Bob said, "Dotson and I had worked a week on the special and they ran it while everybody was at church." [38]

Bob was the first sports anchor to break the story that OU was hiring former Sooner All-American Wade Walker as athletic director in July, 1971. Walker previously had served as head coach and athletic director at Mississippi State University. A member of the selection committee called Bob and said, "Look, you did me a favor once, so now I am paying you back. Wade Walker will be the new athletic director and you can have the story first." [39]

When Bob called the television station with the scoop, news director Ernie Schultz told him not to tell him the news, in fear of other stations hearing the information on the two-way radio. Instead, Bob drove as quickly as he could to the television station and released the story on the noon sportscast. OU regents moved up their official announcement of Walker's selection after Bob reported the story. Later Walker and his wife, Jean, became across-the-street neighbors of the Barrys. Jean and Joan often played cards together. [40]

The Wishbone offense worked magic for OU against Texas in 1971. The Sooners rushed for 435 yards and completed only one pass in a 48-27 victory over the Longhorns. It was Texas Coach Royal's worst defeat of his career. Mildren had 111 yards rushing, but was surpassed by Pruitt who picked up 216 yards on 20 carries and for the second consecutive week was named Associated Press National Back of the Week. Sooner fans threw oranges onto the Cotton Bowl turf, hoping that the Sooners would win the Big Eight title and represent the conference in the Orange Bowl. [41]

After the game, Mildren talked about the Wishbone:
We know it now. It comes natural for us. If I do my job right, and read the option right, we can move it on anybody. And what makes us different than Texas is speed. They mainly have power, but we've got the jets. Today is the high point in my career. It's the greatest I have ever felt after a game. [41]

Bob interviews OU assistant coach Barry Switzer, right, in the Channel Four studios in 1971.

With the Texas win under their belt, OU jumped from No. 8 to No. 2 in the AP poll. The Sooners beat undefeated Colorado the next week and then rushed for an NCAA record of 711 yards against Kansas State in a 75-28 rout. After wins over Iowa State, Missouri, and Kansas, sportswriters began calling the coming matchup between No. 2 Oklahoma and No. 1 Nebraska "the game of the century." [43]

Nebraska had a better defensive team, and playing before a huge national television audience, held Pruitt to just 53 yards on ten carries. Mildren rushed for 130 yards as the lead in the game swapped hands four times. Johnny Rodgers' punt return sparked a late touchdown drive that allowed the Cornhuskers to win the game 35-31, although OU outgained Nebraska 467 to 362 on offense. After the intense game, Bob literally was exhausted from the tension of the slugfest on the field. [44]

OU blasted OSU in the final game of the regular season, 58-14, and beat Auburn in the Sugar Bowl 40-22. Nebraska beat Alabama in the Orange Bowl and Colorado beat Houston in the Astro-Bluebonnet Bowl, setting up a final AP poll with three teams from one conference occupying the top three spots—Nebraska No. 1, Oklahoma No. 2, and Colorado No. 3.

Pruitt finished the season averaging 9.35 yards per carry, still the NCAA record. He was third in the Heisman Trophy balloting. Mildren was the first college quarterback to ever gain more than 1,000 yards on the ground and the first option quarterback to be named All-American. In addition, the Sooners set long-standing records for rushing and total offense.[45]

On his way home from the Sugar Bowl game in New Orleans, Bob reminisced about 11 seasons of broadcasting OU football games. He thought himself lucky to have the job as voice of the Sooners. Little did he know that the security of that position soon would be severely tested.

CHAPTER SIX

Winds of Change

When Bob came to OSU to broadcast our football and basketball games, we welcomed him with open arms.

—MYRON RODERICK

Bob was happy with OU and OU was happy with Bob as the voice of Sooner football and basketball. Network Services owned the exclusive broadcast rights for both sports. Because Lee Allan Smith, KNOR Radio owner Bill Morgan, and Jim Bellatti of Stillwater were the prime movers of Network Services, Bob and Jack Ogle felt secure in their jobs.

However, a series of events in early 1972 removed them from the OU broadcast booth. Network Services surprisingly lost the bid for exclusive rights for OU football and basketball to KTOK Radio in Oklahoma City. The problem arose when Network Services' lawyers prepared a bid that was for "$10 more than the bid of competitors." That clause apparently was illegal and caused Network Services' bid to fail.

Bob and Ogle were so upset by the decision, they visited Oklahoma Attorney General Larry Derryberry to see if anything could be done about the situation. Derryberry remembered, "These were two of my heroes calling games for my alma mater, so I immediately began looking for ways the bid process could be redone." However, Derryberry concluded that the actions of the Network Services' legal counsel had caused the bid to be thrown out. There was nothing Derryberry could do.[1]

KTOK's owners, which included William Schueler and actor Jimmy Stewart, wanted Bob and Ogle to continue to broadcast OU football and basketball games, but there was a problem. KTOK, on the air since 1927, was the chief competition in the Oklahoma City market for WKY-Radio. The two stations often ran one-two in monthly ratings. Edward L. Gaylord, who ran broadcasting operations of the Oklahoma Publishing Company, including WKY-Radio and WKY-TV, was opposed to his news anchor, Ogle, and sports director, Bob, broadcasting OU games live on KTOK. Lee Allan Smith and WKY-TV general manager Norman Bagwell went to bat for Bob and Ogle and at first talked Gaylord into allowing them to continue as the OU broadcast team.

Bob had made little money doing the games for the first 11 years so he proposed to KTOK owners that he be paid what he thought was an exorbitant $40,000 and Ogle receive $30,000 each year. KTOK agreed and Bob thought he "was in tall cotton." Then Gaylord changed his mind and told Smith that a WKY employee could not be on a competing station such as KTOK. To technically comply with Gaylord's mandate, Bob was fired at WKY-TV and rehired on a contract basis to continue his work as sports director. Viewers never knew the difference because Bob was still doing his nightly sportscasts in the 6:00 p.m. and 10:00 p.m. news, weather, and sports blocks.

Gaylord balked at that arrangement, but Bob was allowed to

broadcast OU football games in 1972. Ogle, an established news anchor at WKY-TV, was not permitted to be the color analyst, but was paid extra to host the coach's playback show for OU football. Johnny Keith was hired as color commentator for Bob for the 1972 season. Anticipating that Bob would easily make the transition to KTOK as the voice of the Sooners, Lee Thompson was named producer of the OU broadcasts. Thompson held the post until 1988 although his old friend, Bob, would not be in the booth with him after the 1972 season.[2]

Before football season began, Channel Four sent Bob, news reporter Bob Dotson, and photojournalist Darrell Barton to the Summer Olympics Games in Munich, West Germany, in August and September, 1972, because of heavy Oklahoma involvement. Former OSU men's basketball coach Henry Iba was the coach of the American basketball team and several OSU wrestlers were on the American wrestling squad.

The WKY-TV crew was assigned lodging at the Austrian Alps, a vacation lodge on the West German border with Austria, about 90 miles from Munich. The long drive took too much time each day, so Bob found a small inn about two blocks from the Olympic Village. The inn was owned by Joe Auschwitz and his wife. Auschwitz had fought in the German army under Adolph Hitler and spent much of the war in a prisoner of war camp in Canada where he learned to speak flawless English.[3]

Bob scheduled multiple interviews with Oklahoma-connected coaches and athletes. OCU basketball coach Abe Lemons was president of the United States Basketball Coaches Association and was attending the Summer Games. In an interview, Lemons, known for his funny and outrageous remarks, did not hesitate to spread his good cheer. When Bob asked Lemons what he had to say to folks back home in Oklahoma, he said, "Tell them to stay home. The only ticket I could get was to the hammer throw and I was so far away the crowd would cheer and I would ask, 'How did we do?'" Lemons took Bob to a booth run by a Japanese shoe dealer. Lemons said, "Hey, Bob, all you have to do is to tell the guy you're a coach and he'll give you a pair of shoes." Bob told the Japanese man, "I'm a coach," signed his name as "John MacLeod," the OU basketball coach, and received his shoes, which are still in his closet nearly 40 years later.[4]

There was little security in the Olympic Village, a situation that later would invite disaster. Bob and his crew were able to go in and out of dormitories and offices to do interviews without anyone checking their credentials. On a hot August day, Bob got stuck with a half dozen wrestlers in an Olympic Village elevator. He remembered, "I almost went crazy, claustrophobic, hot, wrestlers banging on the door and cussing in several foreign languages. I thought I was going to die." Finally, after 20 minutes that seemed like 20 hours, Bob and the others were rescued.

Unfortunately, Bob's lasting memories of the Munich Olympic Games are not of sports victories. On the morning of September 5, Bob was awakened by Joe Auschwitz with news that 11 Israeli athletes had been taken hostage in the Olympic Village by Palestinian terrorists who called themselves Black September. Bob, Dotson, and Barton rushed to the Olympic Village that was now surrounded by German soldiers with sub-machine guns and armored cars. Where entry was welcomed before, now soldiers said in English and German, "Get away from this place, go back to your home."[5]

Bob learned to appreciate freedom of the press in America

while covering the Munich Olympics. After the 11 Israeli hostages were killed by terrorists, West German television, which was controlled by the government, reported that everyone was safe. The WKY-TV crew scooped other news organizations with telephone reports of the truth gained through Joe Auschwitz's connections with German police. While the West German government was telling American reporters that no one had been killed, the Oklahoma crew was able to get the real story back to WKY Radio and WKY-TV.[6]

Dotson, one of the most successful television journalists to ever come through Oklahoma, and in 2010 the chief national correspondent for NBC's "Today Show," made an instant name for himself by scooping the world press because the teenage son of the inn owner would run to the top of the inn and report what was happening in the compound where the Israeli hostages were being held. Dotson said, "We were on the air on WKY Radio and NBC Radio for nearly 14 hours. We were able to get the story out by being able to see what was happening from the rooftop and by using the home telephone of Mr. Auschwitz." [7]

After the Olympic Games concluded, the Oklahoma crew headed home. They were asked to strip down to their underwear before boarding an airplane for the trip to Oklahoma City. Bob remembered, "Everybody was scared. We got on the plane not knowing if we would be blown up or what." He was never so glad to be back in the United States. It was a great contrast for him. He arrived back in Oklahoma City less than a week before his first OU football broadcast of the season.[8]

At the end of the 1972 football season, Bob hoped that his big boss, Mr. Gaylord, might allow him to continue to broadcast OU basketball games on KTOK. Bob was still a contract employee for

WKY-TV and was told in no uncertain terms by news director Ernie Schultz that he could not continue to be on the air at Channel Four and do OU basketball. For a couple of days, Bob told Joan that maybe he should quit television and do OU basketball. Joan brought Bob back to the real world when she said, "Look, we can't live on just what you will make out of basketball." Bob returned to WKY-TV the following day, was hired back as a permanent employee, and relinquished the idea of broadcasting OU basketball.[9]

When it was announced that Bob would no longer broadcast OU football games, there was a huge sigh of disappointment from Sooner fans. Marguerite Quinn, an Oklahoma City school of dance owner, wrote "Requiem for a Bob Barry Fan." The poem, which nearly 40 years later hangs in Bob's home office, expressed her sadness at Bob leaving the OU broadcast booth:

I died a little yesterday.
With disbelief I heard them say
That Bob was for another team.
(Awake me from this awful dream!)...[10]

Quinn used the poem to relate how she was introduced to Bob's play-by-play:

One autumn Saturday afternoon
I sat alone here in my room.
Everyone else was at the game,
My solitude was such a shame.
I turned on the radio and heard you say,
"This is Bob Barry...What a beautiful day."
I actually dared you to get me enthused
I really was in an intolerant mood.
But...the longer I listened, the more I was there

And I felt myself gripping the arms of my chair.
Then you yelled "touchdown" for the OU team
And I leaped from my chair with a jubilant scream.[11]

When basketball season began in the early winter of 1972, Bob had withdrawals. For the first time since 1957, he was not preparing for basketball season. Then, he received a call from University of Tulsa (TU) men's basketball coach Jim King. The TU basketball announcer had quit after two games and King was looking for a play-by-play announcer for the Golden Hurricane. Bob accepted the position and began driving to Tulsa for home games in the old state fairgrounds arena.

During the 1972 college basketball season, Bob broadcast University of Tulsa Golden Hurricane games with Sports Information Director Mike Roberts, left, as his color commentator.

Bob knew Coach King because his son, Bobby, had attended King's summer basketball camp for several years. It was a fun year for Bob who took Joan to most of the TU road games where she became close friends with King's wife.

Bob and Joan's boys were growing up. Frank was a very good basketball player and track star. Bobby played on the Norman High School basketball team. Both sons spent a lot of time with their

The Barry family in 1974. Left to right, Joan, Bobby, Bob, and Frank.

Left to right, Bob, comedian Foster Brooks, sports reporter Bob Hurt, and Lincoln Park golf professional U.C. Ferguson at a golf tournament at Quail Creek Golf and Country Club in Oklahoma City in the 1970s.

mother because Bob worked an enormous number of hours each week and traveled to out-of-town football and basketball games. Bobby said, "I never resented that fact, but simply accepted the situation that most of my time was hanging out with Mom." [12]

If Joan and the boys were not at Sterrs Red and White Grocery Store on Main Street, they spent time at Twin Lakes Golf and Country Club east of Norman. In summer months, Joan loved to lay by the pool while the boys swam or played with friends.

Even though the boys rode with Bob to OU home football games, they went their separate ways once inside the stadium. Bob went to the press box to prepare for the radio broadcast and the boys sat in dollar seats in the end zone. After the game, Bobby often scoured through the empty press box looking for left over chocolate chip cookies that had been provided sportswriters and broadcasters by the OU Athletic Department.[13]

One of the first out-of-town basketball trips on which Bob took his sons was to Allen Fieldhouse in Lawrence, Kansas. The Barrys stayed at the Muelbach Hotel in Kansas City, Missouri, the night before the game. Bob was embarrassed in front of his two boys when he locked the keys inside their car at a service station.

Frank and Bobby admired their father and his quest to become the best sportscaster he could be. They saw him on Sunday afternoons in the living room with the curtains closed sitting by a tape recorder listening to and grading his broadcast from the day before. Frank said, "Dad was very critical of himself. He would sit for hours listening to tapes on the old reel-to-reel recorder and then literally give himself a letter grade on the tape box." There were a few Bs, mostly Cs, and a few Ds, but rarely an A.[14]

Bob was well-known in Oklahoma and few people who met Frank and Bobby believed their father was the Bob Barry on radio and television. Frank said, "When I told them who my father was, they said, 'No way!' They thought I was lying to them. I always pointed out that we spelled our name the same, but most kids never believed it."[15]

Frank followed in Bob's footsteps and began playing drums in high school. He has been an active member of bands for most of his adult life. As the older brother, he observed the relationship between his father and mother as an Ozzie and Harriet phenomenon. Frank said, "I never saw them fight. Mother took care of the household and Dad preached his belief that the man of the family must be responsible for taking care of his family financially, no matter how many hours a week he had to work." [16]

Being the sons of one of the state's most popular radio and television personalities certainly caused Frank and Bobby to think about broadcasting careers. As young teens, Frank announced he wanted to be a meteorologist and Bobby said he was going to be "a sports guy." Frank loved science and spent many afternoons in the family garage cooking up some chemical experiment.

Bob told his sons that if they were serious about a career in broadcasting, they needed to start young. Bobby worked at KNOR as a sophomore in high school. He was given one minute each morning to report on the latest news from Norman High. His parents often found him in front of a television watching a football or basketball game with the sound muted, doing his own play-by-play. [17]

After one year in broadcasting at OU, Frank decided his future was not on the air. He changed his major and became a school teacher. Bobby worked at KNOR all through high school and college and graduated with a degree in journalism from OU. During his high school and college days he broadcast Norman High School football games, one year alongside Owen Field public address announcer and WNAD Radio manager Bill Boren. [18]

While Frank was still majoring in broadcasting, he was assigned play-by-play duties of a Norman High School versus Edmond Memorial High School football game on the OU student station, KGOU. While he was in one section of the press box at Owen Field broadcasting the game, Bobby was part of the broadcast team for KNOR in the adjacent booth. After Bob did his 6:00 p.m. sportscast on Channel Four, he drove to the stadium and watched both sons broadcasting the same football game. "It was special," he remembered.[19]

During the spring of 1973, Bob's work at WKY-TV was smooth. However, he wondered how his passion for doing play-by-play of college football and basketball would be satisfied. He was well known throughout the region as a premier radio sports announcer, but most colleges and universities already had contracted with broadcast teams.

Then came a telephone call from Oklahoma State University (OSU) athletic director Floyd Gass who wanted to improve OSU's athletic presence, especially in football, and wanted a high profile play-by-play announcer for statewide radio coverage. He was especially interested in WKY-Radio carrying Cowboy games in Oklahoma City. Because OU games were now broadcast on KTOK Radio, conditions seemed to be ripe for OSU football and basketball to enter the Oklahoma City market on the top-rated radio station.[20]

Oklahoma State University Athletic Director Floyd Gass, left, was a strong supporter of Bob when he became the voice of OSU football and basketball.

Bob, having been "bitten" by a situation where a network, rather than the university, determined who its play-by-play announcers were, sought a different kind of contract with OSU. This time, he and Ogle contracted directly with the OSU Board of Regents as the announcers. However, Bill Platt of KSPI Radio in Stillwater, the former play-by-play announcer for the Cowboys, was still part of the equation.

Platt was a veteran radio announcer who had broadcast for the minor baseball league Oklahoma City Indians and the Ponca City Dodgers. He also was play-by-play announcer for OSU baseball games. A native of Iowa, Platt moved to Oklahoma as a teenager and graduated from Stillwater High School and Oklahoma A & M immediately after World War II. His work at KSPI helped develop the first statewide network of radio stations carrying OSU sporting events.

For two seasons, Bob and Platt alternated quarters of a game with the play-by-play. Whoever was not doing play-by-play served as spotter for the other. When Jack Ogle moved into the booth as Bob's color commentator, Platt became the sideline reporter. A five-time Oklahoma Sportscaster of the Year, Platt was the play-by-play announcer for OSU baseball until 1995.[21] Meanwhile, Mike Treps was hired to broadcast OU football games on KTOK Radio and the Sooner Network.

To improve athletics at OSU, Gass hired a new football coach, Jim Stanley, and hoped for better times for OSU football, which had floundered in the 1960s with nine losing seasons in the decade and only a break-even record of 5-5 in 1969. OSU had not been to a bowl game since 1958. The Cowboys played home football games in Lewis Field, a small facility compared to other Big Eight Conference schools.

Stanley had been defensive coordinator at OSU from 1963 to 1968. A three-year starter for Coach Paul "Bear" Bryant's Texas A & M Aggies in the 1950s, he most recently had coached at Navy and in the Canadian Football League.

Bob always had gotten along well with OSU coaches and athletes during the annual Bedlam game and when he covered OSU wrestling, golf, and other sports for Channel Four. OSU's Labron Harris, Sr., had put together a premier college golf program and OSU's wrestling heritage was second to none. Bob was excited about working with athletic director Gass who he perceived as a forward-thinking man who wanted to do everything in his power to improve OSU's image on fields and courts of competition.

The only unknown was how OSU fans would accept Bob. For a dozen years, he was the voice of the Sooners, and Cowboy fans normally "did not take kindly to OU people dabbling in their business." Bob had only one family connection to OSU—his wife, Joan, was enrolled on the Stillwater campus for a year before she and Bob were married.

The awkwardness of switching from the Sooners to the Cowboys was made easier by Gass and OSU President Robert B. Kamm. Everywhere Bob went, he was cheerfully accepted. Only occasionally did he hear of some caller to an Oklahoma City or Tulsa talk show complaining about a Sooner calling the Aggie football and basketball games.[22]

"I was a part of their family immediately," Bob remembered, "Instead of saying, 'Ugh, a Sooner is doing our games,' they were wonderful to me. They were my friends." OSU officials made a valiant effort to include Joan in pre-game parties and Cowboy celebrations. For the first time, Joan began attending many of the games her husband was broadcasting from high above the field in the press box. Joan often sat in a box with Coach Stanley's wife.

During one game, Bobby Barry came into the box looking for his mother and wearing a tee-shirt with the words, "Choke a Poke—The Sooner the Better." Joan turned Bobby around quickly and ushered him out of the box before Mrs. Stanley could see the shirt.[23]

In addition to Bob, Ogle, and Platt sending the action to listeners on WKY-Radio and other stations around the state on the Cowboy Network, WKY-TV presented a 90-minute film replay of each football game on Sunday nights. Athletic Director Gass had never had his team so prominently displayed to viewers and listeners in the state's largest metropolitan area.

With remarkable depth on the offensive line, an experienced quarterback, and a good tight end, Coach Stanley led his cowboys with enthusiasm. Using the basic Wishbone and pro-set variations, OSU had lopsided wins over Texas-Arlington, Arkansas, and Southern Illinois before losing close games to Texas Tech and Missouri.

The Cowboys finished the year 5-4-2, only the second winning record since the 1950s with linebacker Cleveland Vann named to the Football Writers of America first team and defensive back Alvin Brown was selected first team All-American by *Football News.*[24]

Broadcasting the OU-OSU game certainly was different for Bob in 1973. For the first time in his career, he called the game as the voice of the Cowboys. Even though OSU had not been extremely competitive in the Bedlam Series for more than a decade, the week of the game each year still generated considerable enthusiasm from both teams and their fans. OU was ranked number one in the Associated Press poll, was on its way to a 10-0-1 record, and beat OSU 44-13.

The Bedlam Series had begun in 1904 when Oklahoma A & M met OU on a frozen field at Island Park in Guthrie, Oklahoma. At one time during the game, the wind was so swift that an OSU-punted ball was blown backward through the end zone and into a half-frozen creek. Because a touchdown was at stake, members of both teams dove into the icy waters to recover the ball. OU came up the touchdown, although it would not have mattered. OU won the first Bedlam game 75-0.

With OSU fans feeling better about their football team for 1974, Bob turned his attention to broadcasting OSU basketball games. It had been only three years since the legendary Henry Iba had retired as men's basketball coach for the Cowboys. It had been a long and prestigious run for Iba who led Oklahoma A & M to the NCAA national men's basketball championship in 1945 and 1946, the first team to win back-to-back titles. Iba also coached the American Olympic basketball team to gold medals in 1964 and 1968 and a silver medal in 1972.[25]

When Bob began broadcasting OSU basketball games, the program was in a severe drought that had started in the final years of legendary coach Henry Iba. *Courtesy OSU Athletic Department.*

In the final years before Iba's retirement, OSU basketball's fortunes had dimmed from the glory years. The poor results of the final five years of Iba's tenure were replicated through the 18 years that Bob was the voice of the Cowboy basketball team. In the 1970s and 1980s, OSU had winning records only six times, finished in the top half of the Big Eight Conference only three times and earned a bid to the NCAA Tournament only once.

In 1973, new men's basketball coach Guy R. Strong was hired to bring OSU back to the land of basketball giants. Even a comfortable finish in the Big Eight Conference would suffice. However, even with the efforts of Big Eight scoring champion Kevin Fitzgerald and Andy Hopson, leading rebounder, the Cowboys varsity finished 9-17 and 3-11 in conference.[26]

Olus Holder was the first OSU Cowboy to have 1,000 points and 800 rebounds in a career. *Courtesy OSU Athletic Department.*

With poor performance of the Cowboys basketball team on the court, fan support waned. Later, Coach Strong even canceled his weekly coach's show on WKY-TV because of the inability of the station to find a sponsor for Cowboy basketball. Basketball games were also no longer carried on WKY-Radio.

Bob prepared for the 1974 season with interviews with Coach Stanley and OSU players, including blue-chip running back Terry Miller. Some said the opening game shutout of Wichita State University, 59-0, was a fluke, but national media took note of the Cowboys the following Saturday when OSU beat tenth-ranked Arkansas 26-7. After losses to Baylor, Texas, and Colorado, the Cowboys beat Missouri, Kansas, Kansas State, Iowa State, and nearly spoiled Nebraska's homecoming, eventually losing to the Cornhuskers 7-3.

In the Bedlam game, the Cowboys were on top of number-one-ranked OU in the third quarter. But after a fumble and seven unbelievable minutes of OU offense, the Cowboys were down to the eventual national champion Sooners, 44-13. The 6-5 season record won OSU an invitation to the Fiesta Bowl, the Cowboys' first bowl game in 16 years, to meet Brigham Young University (BYU). In Tempe, Arizona, the Cowboys limited BYU to a pair of first-half field goals in the nationally-televised game won by OSU 16-6. Kenny Walker and Phillip Dokes were named the outstanding offensive and defensive player of the Fiesta Bowl.[27]

CHAPTER SEVEN

Voice of the Cowboys

Bob was the standard for radio play-by-play announcers
in the world of college football.

—GEORGE TOMEK

While Bob was broadcasting OSU football, he still had sub-
stantial contact with OU sports programs by virtue of his job as
Channel Four sports director. Chuck Fairbanks had moved from OU
to the New England Patriots in 1973 and was replaced at the helm
of the Sooners by offensive coordinator Barry Switzer.

Both Bob and Switzer lived in Norman and occasionally ran
into each other at community and university events. Switzer used
his high-powered offense to field exceptional teams in the 1970s,
winning back-to-back national championships in 1974 and 1975. In
1974, the Sooners averaged 43 points a game with Steve Davis at
quarterback, Joe Washington at halfback, and Lucious, Leroy, and
Dewey Selmon on defense. Even though OU won the national title,
the NCAA had placed the Sooners on probation for violations of
rules regarding altering players' high school transcripts and OU was
prohibited from playing in bowl games for two years.

OU fans were bitterly disappointed that the Sooners were not allowed to play in a bowl game. To give OU fans something to cheer about during the bowl season, WKY-TV's Lee Allan Smith came up with the idea of a mythical bowl game between OU and Notre Dame. He approached Bob and Jack Ogle with the idea, and they loved it.[1]

For three weeks, Bob and Ogle worked on a script for the game, called the "Dream Bowl." Smith was able to get ABC sportscaster Howard Cosell to appear as the half-time guest of the dream game. Because the actual interview was by telephone with Cosell at his office at ABC Sports in New York City, Bob had to come up with an explanation for the telephone interview. During half time, Bob said, "We're on the west side of the stadium and Howard Cosell is on the east side, so we are going to do the interview by phone." [2]

The "actors" and "producers" practice for the mythical OU-Notre Dame game broadcast. After the landmark radio production, both houses of the Oklahoma legislature passed congratulatory resolutions. Left to right, Jack Ogle, Lee Allan Smith, Norman Bagwell, _____ and Bob.

The make-believe game occurred in a make-believe stadium, the new Jim Thorpe Stadium in Oklahoma City that seated 100,000 fans. Complete with crowd noise and whistles in the background, Bob and Ogle broadcast each play of the game that ended right for Sooner fans when defensive star Lucious Selmon intercepted a Notre Dame pass and scored a go-ahead touchdown. When the Irish went ahead, the script called for Grant Burget to score the winning touchdown for OU. While Notre Dame was still ahead, a listener called WKY and said, "If Notre Dame wins, you'll pay for it dearly." The mythical game was such a success, the Oklahoma legislature passed a resolution commending Bob, Ogle, Smith, and WKY's Norman Bagwell.[3]

One listener of the mythical broadcast was young Mick Cornett, later a well-known sportscaster, father of the Oklahoma Sports Hall of Fame, and mayor of Oklahoma City. Cornett remembered:

It's one thing to call a game as it happens. It's another to call a game that is not real. During a long Joe Washington run, Bob said, "A whale of a block at the 45." I could see it—and still can. When Lucious Selmon was running an interception back for a touchdown, I was jumping up and down hoping that Bob would get him to the end zone. He did![4]

The mythical game was so well promoted that it interfered with an OU basketball game scheduled for that night at the OU field house. During the football game when Selmon scored the touchdown, fans at the basketball game, listening to OU-Notre Dame on their transistor radios, cheered loudly, totally confusing the players on the basketball court.

In addition to his job as a sports anchor and play-by-play announcer, Bob had other duties at WKY-TV, including assisting Lee

Bob admires a legislative proclamation honoring him for the 1974 broadcast of the mythical OU-Notre Dame football game broadcast on WKY-Radio.

Allan Smith in his production of a giant annual extravaganza known as the *Stars and Stripes Show*, a July Fourth celebration of music and major celebrities that began as a local show and soon was televised nationally as a tribute to America. Smith brought the biggest stars from Hollywood and the music world including Bob Hope, Anita Bryant, and Ed McMahon.

Bob did not mind at all when Smith asked him each year in the 1970s to host sports celebrities when they came to town. Hosting meant picking up the celebrities at the airport, getting them to their hotel, and ushering them around town to special events until it was time for taping the *Stars and Stripes Show*. Sports figures who appeared on the program were Roger Staubach, Johnny Unitas, Steve Owens, Mickey Mantle, Don Klosterman, Bear Bryant, Barry Switzer, Bud Wilkinson, and Hall of Fame pitcher Bob Feller. Bob was especially pleased when he was able to host Mantle, Bryant, and his childhood hero, Feller. He was able to spend time with the larger-than-life heroes and often ate meals with them.[5]

Before the 1975 football season, OSU football coach Stanley told Bob that he was installing a new offense, the slot I, to complement his Wishbone formation that had brought him more victories

Terry Miller was a high school star in Colorado before becoming a two-time All-American at OSU in 1976 and 1977. His number 43 is one of three retired numbers at OSU. *Courtesy OSU Athletic Department.*

in his first two seasons than any other Cowboys coach before him. At a pre-game rally broadcast on several radio stations, Bob interviewed Stanley and running back Terry Miller, who wished that the nagging injuries that throttled his success the year before would go away. Stanley said, "If we play as well as we can every game—I'm talking about playing at a fever pitch—everything will take care of itself."[6]

When Cowboys fans recognized Bob at restaurants or public events, they expressed optimism to him about the Cowboys. A magazine noticed that "spirit at OSU is reaching an all-time high with the advent of a new, shattering Cowpoke yell—Orange Power!"[7]

OSU opened the 1975 season with the program's 300th victory, a 34-0 whipping of Wichita State University, then won every non-conference game for the first time in 30 years. Mistakes cost OSU several conference games and the Cowboys finished the season at 7-4, but there was no bowl game invitation.

Terry Miller was a junior in 1976 and already was approaching Bob Fenimore's rushing records. Before the season, Bob sensed a special unity in the Cowboy grid team. Abby Daigle was back as a deadly placekicker. Cliff Parsley was trying to lead the Big Eight in punting for the fourth consecutive year. Charlie Weatherbie's "rifle-like" passing arm was complemented by backfield skills of Miller, Robert Turner, and Skip Taylor.

The Bedlam game was in the middle of the season for the first time. In October, OSU played a near perfect game and beat OU 31-24. It was the first win over the Sooners since 1966. With an 8-3 regular season record, OSU played BYU in the Tangerine Bowl and easily beat the Cougars 49-21.[8]

In 1976, the Gaylord family sold WKY-TV to the company that owned the *Detroit Evening News*. It was the first time Oklahoma's first television station was owned by owners who were not Oklahomans. New ownership changed Channel Four's call letters to KTVY and bought newspaper advertisements that said, "What's in a name? Our people are the same." The ads pointed out that even though WKY-TV had a new name, viewers still could expect excellence in local news, weather, and sports, especially during the state's most widely-viewed 10:00 p.m. news program with George Tomek, Jim Williams, and Bob.

Tomek, a graduate of the University of Tulsa, was a familiar face and voice to Oklahomans. He had worked with Bob in the late 1960s, especially on the Sunday night show before Bob became sports director and went fulltime with Channel Four. After stints as a news anchor in St. Louis and Dallas, Tomek returned to Channel Four as a prime-time anchor.

"Bob was the kindest and nicest person anyone ever wanted to be around," Tomek remembered. "I am sure he had his ups and downs of life like all of us, but he never displayed it professionally. He was the same all the time, with a smile and a friendly greeting no matter how early or how late it was in the day."[9]

Tomek often scanned the wire services and magazines for a funny story to use at the end of a show. He could always count on Bob to laugh almost uncontrollably at his story, making it real for audiences.[10]

On one occasion, the news director changed the studio set. A black set featured the news anchor in the foreground and the sports and weather anchors to the left and right in the background. Sports and weather could control their own lights and would turn them on when it was their time to go on the air. As each of the anchors completed their time, the lights were turned off. On Halloween night, Bob had his sports desk lights flashing on and off and participated in a very funny ghoulish exchange with Tomek.[11]

When Tomek turned 40 years old, the on-the-air talent at Channel Four put together a gag video for a birthday party. The highlight was Bob trying to emulate Tomek as an over-the-hill, 40-year-old news anchor. Tomek remembered, "After starting to nod off a few times reading a script, Bob let his head hit the desk, making like he had fallen sound asleep. What a ham!" [12]

Bob had his own gag reel for station parties and other events. One of his favorite "pretend" reports was him doing a stand-up report at Owen Field when a dozen cheerleaders converged upon him and began kissing him and running their fingers through his hair. None of the gag reels ever made it on the air.[13]

In 1976, KTVY management sent Bob to cover the Summer Olympic Games in Montreal, Quebec, Canada. Bob found a great deal of contrast between Montreal and the Olympics four years earlier in Munich. Because of the Munich massacre of Israeli athletes, security in Montreal was unbelievable. Bob also found the people in Montreal less friendly than in West Germany. His explanation was that the French-speaking people in Quebec were "put out" when they had to speak English to American reporters.[14]

The Montreal Olympics featured 14-year-old Nadia Comaneci of Romania scoring seven perfect 10s and winning three gold medals in gymnastics. When Bob watched the young girl make Olympic history, he had no idea that she would someday marry OU gymnast Bart Conner and make her home only a mile or two from Bob's home in Norman.[15]

Bob also was intrigued with the best American boxing team ever assembled for Olympic competition. Sugar Ray Leonard, Michael Spinks, Leon Spinks, Leo Randolph, and Howard Davis, Jr., all won gold medals. All but Davis eventually won world professional championships.[16]

In 1976, 22 radio stations made up the Cowboy Sports Network for OSU football games. Bob was joined on the broadcasts by Bill Platt, right. Note both announcers' white shoes. *Courtesy Oklahoma State University Athletic Department.*

Bob prepares to throw out the first pitch at an Oklahoma City 89ers baseball game at All Sports Stadium. Unfortunately, Bob "bounced the ball in front of the plate."

Before the 1977 football season, there were rumors that Bob would return to OU as the play-by-play announcer. It was well known that OU Regents had vetoed the Oklahoma News Network's plans for Mike Treps to return as the voice of the Sooners. There also was a newspaper story that indicated that Bob was the only announcer the regents could agree upon to replace Treps. When Bob said no to OU, Gary Johnson of KXYZ Radio in Houston was hired, although he had not done play-by-play for five years since leaving the post as lead announcer for the University of New Mexico radio broadcasts.[17]

Terry Miller's senior season in 1977 was phenomenal as he became the first OSU player to be named Big Eight Conference Player of the Year. Miller had 27 games of gaining more than 100 yards in his career and finished the season as the third-best runner in the nation. Bob watched Miller's career closely because he always believed he helped recruit Miller to OSU. Before Miller chose OSU, he was at Channel Four on a tour because he was interested in broadcasting. When he asked Bob about OSU football, Bob "went on and on" about the coaching staff and Cowboys commitment to excellence.[18]

In 1977, Miller led the Big Eight in rushing, total offense, and all-purpose yardage. A two-time All-American, he was second in the Heisman Trophy balloting to the winner, running back Earl Campbell of Texas. Miller later played four years in the NFL for Buffalo and Seattle.[19]

Miller's dominance in the backfield increased attendance at OSU home games at the newly-refurbished Lewis Field. In five home games in 1977, the crowd averaged 46,577, thousands more than in previous seasons. Miller's personal accomplishments overshadowed the Cowboys' 4-7 season record.

Leadership at the top of OSU changed in 1977 when Dr.
Lawrence L. Boger became the institution's 14th president. A native
of Indiana, Boger had earned degrees from Purdue University and
Michigan State University where he served as Provost and Vice
President of Academic Affairs immediately before he was hired as
president of OSU. Boger and his wife, Frances June Boger, made
Bob and Joan feel like they were an integral part of the OSU family
at both official functions and private gatherings. Bob said, "They
became good friends. Dr. Boger always wanted to know how he
could help make my job better." [20]

President Boger conceived the idea to use Bob for more than
just a play-by-play announcer. Bob was invited to represent the
university at rallies and alumni functions. In essence, he became an
unofficial public relations representative for OSU.

In Bob's busy life, he always found time to play golf with
friends for fun or in charity tournaments. His great rounds or poor
rounds sometimes made the newspaper in columns by sportswriters
with whom he played. In December, 1977, Bob Hurt wrote in his
column on the sports page of *The Daily Oklahoman* about perfect
Christmas gifts for sports fans. He mentioned that Lake Hefner's
golf course was selling special Molitar golf balls for $2 each. How-
ever, Hurt recommended against buying the special, serialized golf
ball. Hurt wrote, "It takes about two hours longer to play a round
since friend Bob Barry got one. He can't afford to lose it." [21]

On another occasion, Hurt wrote about the famous story of Bob
not being able to identify the Barry family lawn mower. Bob was
rarely home during daylight hours, so Joan had mowed the family yard for years. When Joan asked Bob to pick up the mower at a
repair shop, the owner asked, "Which mower is yours?" Bob was

embarrassed when he admitted he had no earthly idea which mower was his. Hurt told the story in his daily column:

> *He couldn't identify the mower. He's never used one. Never.*
> *Ever. Claims it was part of the marriage contract. Guess that's*
> *why grass keeps growing under the feet. Or, maybe why he has*
> *such grass roots support.* [22]

BELOW: In the late 1970s, Bob contracted to do the play-by-play for weekly college basketball games for TVS, a network based in New York City. Bob's broadcast partner for the games was former Iowa State University basketball star Gary Thompson, left.

ABOVE: Frank Barry receives his bachelor's degree from the University of Oklahoma in May, 1978.

In 1978, OSU hired a new men's basketball coach, Jim "Killer" Killingsworth, who had produced an excellent winning record at Cerritos Junior College in California and at Idaho State University where he captured the Big Sky Conference championship. Historian Doris Dellinger wrote, "But the OSU program had slipped too far to be resuscitated in a season, and when his Cowboys went 10-16, Killingsworth endured his first losing season in 19 years as a cage coach." [23]

The only difference in the OSU basketball program was that games could now be heard on more than KSPI in Stillwater. Bob began broadcasting OSU basketball games on the Cowboy Sports Network.

There were other changes at OSU in 1978. Floyd Gass resigned as athletic director after eight years at the post. At a press conference announcing his resignation, Gass conceded that outside pressures, including an NCAA investigation of a secret club of backers in the football program, contributed to his decision to step down.[24]

OSU Regents moved quickly to fill the vacancy. Dr. Richard A. "Dick" Young was named athletic director at OSU. He had held the same position at Bowling Green State University since 1971.

Coach Jim Stanley fielded a Cowboys football team that could not get untracked for its first five games in 1978. All-American running back Terry Miller was gone and it was difficult to operate under a two-year probation by the NCAA. Bob called the action as the Cowboys lost to Wichita State, Florida State, Arkansas, North Texas, and Kansas State. Weary of nine consecutive losses dating back to the previous season, the Cowboys finally beat Colorado at Lewis Field.

With a disappointing season, many fans called for Stanley's job. In six years he compiled a 35-31-2 record and had taken the Cowboys to two bowl games. However, the NCAA investigation and a losing record brought about his release from contract.[25]

In December, Bob broke the story that OSU had chosen 35-year-old Jimmy Johnson as the new football coach. Athletic Director Young confirmed the story the following day when Johnson was introduced as the new head coach. Johnson had been reluctant to apply for the job at OSU for the task of rebuilding the troubled program. He was the final applicant interviewed by regents who liked his coaching sharpness and winning attitude. He was nicknamed "Jimmy Jumpup" because he never stayed on the ground for long during football practices or games.[26]

After playing college football at the University of Arkansas where he played with future Dallas Cowboys owner Jerry Jones on the 1964 national championship team, Johnson was an assistant football coach at Louisiana Tech University, Wichita State University, OU, Arkansas, and the University of Pittsburgh. At Arkansas, he had hoped to become head coach to replace retiring Frank Broyles, although Johnson was passed over when Lou Holtz was hired to lead the Razorbacks.

The first time Bob met Johnson, as an assistant coach at OU years before, he was impressed by his enthusiasm. Johnson and other OU coaches dressed up in costume each Halloween and appeared at many homes in Norman, including the Barry home on Thorton Drive. Bob and Joan normally invited the coaches in for a short visit before the costumed throng left for another Halloween visit.

As the new OSU head coach, Johnson sat down with Bob and "picked his brain" about OSU fans and support among alumni and businesses in the state. Johnson knew that if he was to build a successful program on the gridiron, he must have the backing of prominent OSU supporters.[27]

With OSU fans getting excited about prospects for the next football season, they were less than enthralled about the continuing lack of success for the OSU men's basketball team. Coach Killingsworth added junior college prospects and the Oklahoma high school Player of the Year, Matt Clark, but shooting slumps, turnovers, and injuries brought down the Pokes in a 12-15 season. Despite installation of new lights to brighten the court in Gallagher Hall, it was a dim season. While riding to a game at Iowa State on a school bus with the team, Killingsworth told Bob, "I'm tired of this league. I'm leaving as soon as I can." [28] In March, 1979, Killingsworth became head coach at Texas Christian University and Paul Hansen, the well-known and well-loved coach and athletic director at Oklahoma City University, was asked to rebuild OSU's cage reputation. [29]

The Barrys with friends at dinner in 1979. Left to right, Jody McCall, Don Symcox, Bob, Joan, Tom McCall, and Mary Louise Symcox.

Bob often was invited to speak to civic clubs and church groups about sports in general. In September, 1979, he participated in a five-day workshop on sports broadcasting at Central State University in Edmond. Bob's topic was "How to become a sportscaster." He had specific advice for broadcasting students who thought they might want a career in radio and television sports. Bob said, "If you are not an enthusiastic sports fan, you probably should consider another occupation." Bob admitted that a sportscaster's job was not as glamorous as it might appear, but was filled with hard work and long hours. [30]

Bob also told students at Central State that a good foundation for a sportscaster came after years of going to games, reading books, devouring the day's sports pages, and listening to radio and television broadcasts. "Once you are involved in broadcasting," he said, "you must practice constantly. Go to little league or high school games and practice play-by-play. Turn the sound down on television and do your own play-by-play." [31]

Bob also said students interested in sportscasting should be willing to start at the bottom, doing any game anywhere, no matter how unimportant or unchallenging. He also encouraged future play-by-play announcers to listen critically to other announcers. "Don't copy somebody else's style," he said, "but be a good listener and pick up a good system of do's and don'ts from other announcers. If you hear a good technique, add it to your style." [32]

Excitement was running high in Stillwater as Coach Jimmy Johnson's Cowboys football team prepared for the 1979 season. In a pre-season interview with Bob on Channel Four, Johnson said, "I like to have a good time. On the field I like to whoop and holler and yell. When it comes to playing ball, I want my players to have fun and win and convince other good players to come be part of us." [33]

Johnson surrounded himself with a young and enthusiastic coaching staff that would produce several successful head coaches later in their careers. Assistant coaches included Pat Jones, Dave Wannstedt, Butch Davis, Bill Miller, and Bum Phillips. Pat Jones said, "Hiring Jimmy helped OSU image-wise. You put OU coach Barry Switzer in front of a camera and you put Jimmy Johnson in front of a camera, and the game is on. I think from an image standpoint, Jimmy lit Stillwater up." [34]

When OSU assistant coaches gathered, many brought their children. Bob occasionally had conversations with Phillips' young son, Wade, later a successful NFL coach and head coach of the Dallas Cowboys.

With a potent passing game and a defense inspired by junior defensive end Dexter Manley and linebacker Rick Antle, the Cowboys headed into a 7-4 season. All four losses were to teams that were bound for bowl appearances. Injuries stacked up each week. In September, Tom Dirato wrote in the *Oklahoma Journal*, "The training room looked like a battlefield infirmary. The players were literally assigned numbers Sunday as they arrived for early morning treatment." [35]

With five conference victories, OSU placed third in the Big Eight Conference and Johnson was named Big Eight Coach of the Year by the Associated Press and United Press International.

As basketball season began, Bob renewed his longtime friendship with new OSU basketball coach Paul Hansen. He had known Hansen when he coached at OCU, both as a longtime assistant to the legendary Abe Lemons and as head coach of the Chiefs. Hansen had a life won-loss record of 499-211, but almost everyone assumed the Cowboys would occupy the bottom half of the Big Eight Conference.

In an interview with Hansen, Bob asked about the behind-the-scenes job of recruiting fine players for OSU. Hansen was quick to define his recruiting practice. He told Bob, "I don't cheat. I don't buy clothes or tires for their cars. If that's what a player wants, he's got the wrong man." [36]

Early in the season, forward Don Youman and guard Matt Clark were injured and two other players were declared academically ineligible. On November 30, the Cowboys gave Hansen his 500th career win with a 102-47 whipping of Texas Wesleyan University. Ed Odom led the Big Eight in scoring but OSU ended the season 10-17.

CHAPTER EIGHT

Veteran Sportscaster

*Bob comes across on the air as a friendly guy who
could be your next door neighbor.*

—ROSS PORTER

By 1980, Bob had been a radio play-by-play announcer for
24 years, with 20 years as the voice of football and basketball at
Oklahoma's two largest universities. He had unprecedented coop-
eration at both OSU and OU. He was the voice of the Cowboys
and enjoyed splendid support from the athletic department, football
coach Jimmy Johnson, basketball coach Paul Hansen, and President
Boger. Bob lived in Norman, knew Barry Switzer and his coaching
staff, and considered OU athletic department administrators among
his friends.

Before the 1980 football season, Bob signed a new three-year
contract with OSU to continue to broadcast football and basketball
games. When the contract extension was announced, Athletic Director Dick Young said, "I know I speak for the entire university in
expressing our delight over Bob's desire to continue our games." [1]

Bob, who was named Sportscaster of the Year in Oklahoma
for the eighth time, said he was "tremendously happy" to be part of

the OSU athletic family and was "eagerly looking forward to many more years of association with Oklahoma State." [2]

OSU also renewed the contract with WKY-Radio for the station to continue as the flagship station of the Oklahoma State Football Network. A.D. "Dee" Sadler, WKY-Radio general manager and Bob's friend since high school, was happy that his station would continue to broadcast football and basketball games in the Oklahoma City market. [3]

Bob is congratulated by State Senator Herschal Crow of Altus in 1980 for outstanding service as the voice of the Oklahoma State University Cowboys.

At halftime of an OSU basketball game, Bob is joined by his fellow on-the-air personalities at KFOR-TV. Front row, left to right, Linda Cavanaugh, Bob, and Devon Scillian. Back row, Dan Threlkeld and Teresa Green.

Bobby Barry graduated from the University of Oklahoma in May, 1980, with a bachelor's degree in education.

OSU was picked to finish third in the Big Eight Conference football race in 1980. However, after a disappointing season-opening loss to West Texas State University, there was a quarterback controversy, especially after walk-on quarterback John Doerner broken his fibula. Houston Nutt and Jim Traber were Doerner's backups and competed for the job. Nutt later became head coach at Arkansas and Mississippi and Traber, after a major league baseball career, became a popular sports radio talk show host in Oklahoma City.[4] Capping a tough 4-7 season, the Cowboys lost in Norman to sixth-ranked OU 63-14.

Where football fortunes were down, OSU basketball hopes were rising. The popular coach Paul Hansen opened the 1980-1981 season 16-3 with attendance at Gallagher Hall up more than 2,000 per game from the previous season. Eddie "Half-Court" Hannon made a 45-foot shot to upset defending national champion Louisville 72-71 before a huge crowd at Gallagher. For the first time in 24 years, OSU played in the prestigious All-College Tournament in Oklahoma City, the oldest holiday tournament in the nation. Matt Clark was the tournament Most Valuable Player.

By mid-season, OSU was ranked 19th in the country and was the fourth-highest scoring team in the NCAA. Abruptly, conference losses began piling up and Hansen's squad ended the season at 18-9. The Cowboys were fifth in the Big Eight. In an interview with Bob, Hansen took the blame for the losing streak and declined a bid to the NIT, even though he was named Big Eight Conference Coach of the Year by the Associated Press.[5]

One of Jimmy Johnson's goals as football coach at OSU was to create a positive attitude and generate enthusiasm among writers and broadcasters who covered Cowboys football. He had his work cut out dealing with newspaper reporters who did not acknowledge OSU until they won at least six games in a season. "But I had no problems with Bob Barry," Johnson said. "From the beginning at OSU, Bob felt the excitement we were trying to generate. When we won big games, he conveyed the excitement to our fans perfectly. Everything was upbeat about his play-by-play description and his reporting about our program on his nightly sportscast."[6]

LISTEN TO
OKLAHOMA STATE UNIVERSITY
COWBOY FOOTBALL
EVERY SATURDAY ON WKY
Brought to you by . . .
McDonald's Restaurants in the greater Oklahoma City area,
Fred Jones Industries
Fidelity Bank Oklahoma
Association of Electric Cooperative

BOB BARRY
Play-by-play

ROBBIE ROBERTSON
Color

OSU

WKY RADIO 930

In 1981, WKY-TV sportscaster Robbie Robertson joined Bob to broadcast OSU football games on the Oklahoma State Football Network. *Courtesy Oklahoma Publishing Company.*

Johnson allowed Bob to have incredible access, even on game day. Other football coaches had insisted on taping pre-game shows on Thursday or Friday before a Saturday game. However, Johnson was so calm on the morning of a Saturday afternoon game that he allowed Bob to bring his tape recorder to his office and tape the pre-game show just hours before kickoff.[7]

In 1981, the Cowboys were 7-5 with wins over Louisville, Missouri, and Kansas State. With Oklahoma City's Rusty Hilger at quarterback, OSU accepted an invitation to play Texas A & M in the Independence Bowl in Shreveport, Louisiana. After the bowl bids were handed out, OSU lost to OU 27-3. Then the Cowboys lost to Texas A & M 33-16 in the bowl game. The Cowboys finished third in the Big Eight for the second time in three years.[8]

A change for Bob's broadcasts of OSU football games was a new color analyst in 1982. Tom Dirato, a former newspaper writer for the *Oklahoma Journal*, had been helping Bob broadcast OSU basketball games since 1977. Dirato also became director of radio and television operations in the OSU athletic department and hosted more than 400 coaches shows and was on the air for literally hundreds of OSU basketball and baseball games.

Before the 1982 football season Coach Johnson visited at length with Bob about how "things were turning around" at OSU. The Cowboys were off probation, up to their maximum 95 scholarships, and had built a solid foundation to enable OSU to compete more effectively in the Big Eight Conference and recruit blue chip players in Oklahoma and Texas. Johnson made staff changes, putting Pat Jones in charge of the OSU offense and naming Dave Wannstedt as defensive coordinator. In addition, the 1982 season saw the introduction of running back Ernest Anderson and defensive player Leslie O'Neal.[9]

Anderson opened the season with 220 yards, the first of four 200-yard games on his way to leading the nation in rushing and setting a new school record of 1,877 yards, the fifth best in NCAA history. In a hot and cold season, OSU had a 4-5-2 record. Bob believed the Cowboys were a better team than their record, but an average of more than three turnovers a game highlighted a dismal season.[10]

In 1982, Bob lost two sportscasters at Channel Four within a two-week period. Kerry Addington took a job at KPRC-TV in Houston and Ron Thulin resigned to accept a position as the number two sports talent at KXAS-TV in Dallas. Thulin had been at KTVY for seven years and had hosted *The Barry Switzer Show* and the *OU Playback Show* on Channel Four.[11]

One of the first applicants for the vacant positions in the KTVY sports department was Bob's son, Bobby, who had experience as a sportscaster at KAUT-TV in Oklahoma City and at the CBS affiliate in Wichita Falls, Texas. Bobby sent an audition tape to his father and KTVY general manager Lee Allan Smith.[12]

Quickly, Smith offered the job to Bobby. However, Smith was concerned about viewers confusing two sportscasters who both went by the name "Bob Barry." Even though Bobby was not actually a "junior," Smith decided from that moment on, Bobby would be known professionally as "Bob Barry, Jr." Nearly three decades later, Bobby is still "Bob Barry, Jr.," "BBJ," or "Junior" on radio and television.[13]

BBJ began doing sports reports and anchoring the weekend sports shows. Robbie Robertson was the anchor in the early morning and at noon. Bob still anchored the 5:00 p.m., 6:00 p.m., and 10:00 p.m. sports shows.

The first week for BBJ on the job was difficult. His father went to Scotland on vacation and Robertson left for a trip to Las Vegas, Nevada. BBJ was left alone in the sports department with brand new employee, Robert Allen. For a week, BBJ anchored the 5:00 a.m., 6:00 a.m., noon, 5:00 p.m., 6:00 p.m., and 10:00 p.m. sportscasts. He slept in the Channel Four green room because his 20-hour work day did not give him time to return home for any quality sleep. BBJ was "extremely happy" when Bob and Robertson resumed their normal schedules the following week.[14]

BBJ received lots of advice from his father as to how to be a great sportscaster. "His main advice was to play it straight. Let the event be the story, you don't need to be the story," BBJ said. Bob believed that announcers should never be bigger than the event and that gurus and analysts who came with cable television sports crossed the line and tried to become the story rather than describing a game, an athlete, or a coach.[15]

Bob also had advice for his sportscaster son for how to handle the demanding hours of the profession. BBJ recognized that his father was not home much of the time when he was growing up and has tried to take advantage of every opportunity to spend an hour at home. BBJ said, "Even if it is between shows, and only for an hour, Dad advised me to go home."[16]

Bob's life as the voice of the Cowboys changed in 1983 when Myron Roderick returned to Stillwater as athletic director at OSU. Roderick, a three-time national champion as a Cowboy wrestler, was only 23 when he won the first of several national wrestling championships for OSU. His Cowboy wrestlers dominated the sport for 13 years from 1957 to 1969 and captured seven NCAA crowns. After coaching, Roderick was the first executive director of the

United States Wrestling Federation and launched the campaign to eventually build the National Wrestling Hall of Fame in Stillwater.

Bob and Joan became close friends with Roderick and his wife, Joann. "We were made to feel so close to OSU," Bob said. The Barrys were included in OSU functions, both athletic and non-athletic events. Roderick knew how popular Bob was in the Oklahoma City television market and around the state as the voice of the Cowboys. He asked Bob to accompany coaches and players on caravan trips to speak to booster clubs and Cowboy supporters. Often, Roderick sent a private plane to Oklahoma City to transport Bob to highly-publicized events from McAlester to Altus and Miami to Enid.[17]

In 1983, Jimmy Johnson hired several new coaches for the OSU football program, including Larry Coker, who later would win a national championship at the University of Miami. Johnson and his staff built a new defensive scheme that later traveled from Stillwater to Miami to professional football, a "built-for-speed" defense that was anchored by Cowboys John Washington, Leslie O'Neal, and Rodney Harding, one of the greatest pass-rush trios in Big Eight Conference history.[18]

OSU began the 1983 football season 4-0 for the first time since 1975 before meeting top-ranked Nebraska and 15th-ranked OU. *Sports Illustrated* called the 1983 Nebraska squad "the best team in college football history." Turner Gill was the quarterback and eventual Heisman Trophy winner Mike Rozier was the running back. The Cornhuskers had beaten their opponents by an average score of 58-11 before their game with OSU.[19]

Coach Johnson said his game plan was to do anything to slow down the Nebraska offense. Assistant Coach Pat Jones remembered, "We practiced calling either the Tiger Blitz or Corner Fire

At Christmas, 1980, left to right, Joan's mother, Ruth Philpin, Bob, and Bob's mother, Frances Barry.

Bob and Joan on one of their many trips to Caesar's Palace in Las Vegas, one of their favorite out-of-town destinations.

every down." On the first two plays, the Cowboys held Rozier to a five-yard loss and sacked the quarterback. Jones said, "The Big Red Machine had been hit in the teeth. Everyone in the place stood up." [20]

The Cowboys led Nebraska 10-7 at halftime and sent shock-waves around the country before eventually losing to the Cornhuskers 14-10. Nebraska went undefeated in the regular season and played the University of Miami in the Orange Bowl for the national championship.

For the OSU players, coaches, and Bob's broadcast staff, the game against Nebraska was emotionally draining. After nearly upsetting the Cornhuskers, how could OSU bounce back the following week against Bedlam foe OU? In the pre-game show, Coach Johnson told Bob that defense could make the difference and that his players would not let the emotion of the previous week diminish their effort against the Sooners.

OSU started well, building a 20-3 lead over OU in the first half and maintaining the margin into the first minute of the fourth quarter. OU had converted only two of 15 third downs. Then bad things began happening to OSU. Two defensive backs ran together and gave up a 73-yard touchdown pass. OU recovered an onside kick, scored 18 points in the final 10 minutes of the game and beat OSU 21-20. It was a "Bedlam heartbreak" for the Cowboy faithful.

Four games were lost by a total of 12 points in 1983. The Cowboys' defense was eighth nationally against the rush and first in interceptions and turnover ratio. With an 8-4 record, OSU was invited to play in the Bluebonnet Bowl on New Year's Eve and beat Baylor 24-14, largely on the quarterbacking of Rusty Hilger and running of All-American Ernest Anderson.

Even before the Bluebonnet Bowl game, Bob was reporting on his nightly sportscast about rumors that OSU football coach Johnson was looking at other jobs. He had been a finalist for the head coaching position at Rice University and interviewed at the University of Arkansas. Then, when Howard Schnellenberger resigned at the University of Miami, speculation was rampant that Johnson would take that job. Bob talked to Myron Roderick and other OSU officials and reported that if Miami offered Johnson the job, he would go.[21]

When Johnson was hired at Miami, assistant head coach Pat Jones openly admitted to Bob and his friends that he wanted to be head coach of the Cowboys. The first person Jones talked to was retired OSU basketball coach Henry Iba who told him, "Don't try to

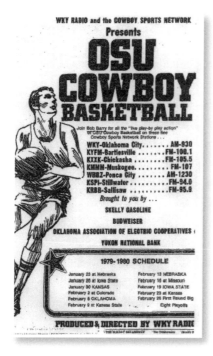

WKY RADIO and the COWBOY SPORTS NETWORK
Presents

OSU COWBOY BASKETBALL

Join Bob Barry for all the "live play-by play action" of OSU Cowboy Basketball on these fine Cowboy Sports Network Stations . . .

WKY-Oklahoma City	AM-930
KYFM-Bartlesville	FM-100.1
KXXK-Chickasha	FM-105.5
KMMM-Muskogee	FM-107
WBBZ-Ponca City	AM-1230
KSPI-Stillwater	FM-94.0
KRBB-Sallisaw	FM-95.9

Brought to you by . . .

SKELLY GASOLINE
BUDWEISER
OKLAHOMA ASSOCIATION OF ELECTRIC COOPERATIVES
YUKON NATIONAL BANK

1979-1980 SCHEDULE

January 23 at Nebraska	February 13 NEBRASKA
January 26 at Iowa State	February 16 at Missouri
January 30 KANSAS	February 19 IOWA STATE
February 2 at Colorado	February 23 at Kansas
February 6 OKLAHOMA	February 26 First Round Big
February 9 at Kansas State	Eight Playoffs

PRODUCED & DIRECTED BY WKY RADIO

In the 1980s, Bob broadcast OSU basketball games on seven state radio stations, including flagship station, WKY-Radio in Oklahoma City. *Courtesy Oklahoma Publishing Company.*

get the job through the media. Let your friends get the job for you." That strategy worked and Jones was hired as head football coach for the 1984 season. The only assistant coach Jones lost was Butch Davis who became Johnson's defensive line coach at Miami. It was a good career choice, because Davis later became head coach of the Hurricanes.[22]

OSU received an unexpected dividend by playing in the 1983 Bluebonnet Bowl in Houston. A high school senior in the Houston area, Thurman Thomas, attended nearly every Cowboy practice because he wore the same number 34 as OSU running back Ernest Anderson. Butch Davis and Willie Anderson led the recruiting effort for Thomas, one of the finest running backs produced by Texas high schools. Bob was aware early in the recruiting season that if high school standouts such as Thomas would commit to OSU, 1984 would be a special season. Thomas did commit, and 1984 was special.

The Cowboys were unranked at the beginning of the season but opened against Arizona State University in Tempe, Arizona. Bob, color analyst Tom Dirato, and the broadcast crew flew to Arizona two days early to soak up some sunshine and get ready for the game against the Sun Devils who had been picked by *Sport* Magazine to win the national championship. On the field, OSU beat Arizona State 45-3 and the Cowboys jumped to Number 12 in the Associated Press weekly poll.[23]

Bob and his radio broadcast team were working for a new boss in 1984. Learfield Communications of Jefferson City, Missouri, won the contract to broadcast OSU football and basketball games on the Cowboy Sports Network. Learfield was founded in 1972 as the Missouri Network, Inc., by Clyde Lear and Derry Brownfield. What began as a small farm network heard on six radio stations in Missouri became a diverse media enterprise with hundreds of employees. Learfield entered the sports market in 1975 by broadcasting University of Missouri football and basketball. By 1984, Learfield owned broadcast rights for the University of Kansas, University of Missouri, Iowa State University, University of Illinois, St. Louis Cardinals, and Kansas City Royals.[24]

After wins against Bowling Green University and San Diego State University, OSU moved into the top 10 of the AP poll for the first time since 1945. When the Cowboys traveled to Lincoln to play Nebraska, both teams were in the top ten and the game was selected as the ABC Game of the Week with announcers Keith Jackson and Frank Broyles. OSU led 3-0 at halftime but lost the game 17-3. Even with the loss, the Cowboys managed to stay in the AP Top Ten.

In a win over Kansas State, Thurman Thomas began showing what a brilliant star he would become. Entering the game on the third series, Thomas rushed for 206 yards and scored two touchdowns. Secretly, Coach Jones told Bob that he and his staff were struggling with moving Thomas ahead of starter, Charles Crawford.

After Jimmy Johnson coached at OSU, be moved to the National Football League and coached the Dallas Cowboys and Miami Dolphins. *Courtesy OSU Athletic Department.*

Leslie O'Neal was a two-time All-American defensive tackle at OSU in 1984 and 1985. A first-round draft choice, he played 14 years for the San Diego Chargers in the NFL. *Courtesy OSU Athletic Department.*

Following wins over Missouri and Iowa State, the national media began descending upon Stillwater. It was a magical time for the school and for Bob, whose telephone occasionally rang with inquiries from sportswriters and sportscasters. The *New York Times* and *Sports Illustrated* published special reports on the Cowboys' success.

In the Bedlam game, OSU was ranked Number 2 and OU was Number 3 in the United Press International poll. The rankings were reversed in the AP poll. Regardless, it was a huge game. Coach Jones said, "Basically, we were in a two-game playoff for the national championship. The winner of the Bedlam game was going to the Orange Bowl to plead the case for the national title." [25]

It was the biggest Bedlam game to date in the storied rivalry. Bob was apprehensive as he arrived at Owen Field early. "It was not just another game," he remembered. "I had called hundreds of high school and college games from that press box, but this game was very different. Even though I had been the voice of the Sooners for years and now had even more time invested as the voice of the Cowboys, there was a special air of excitement that literally hung over the field as the fans filed into the stadium and the players nervously ran from the tunnel onto the playing surface." [26]

Just before halftime, Rusty Hilger threw a fade route to Jamie Harris for an OSU touchdown, a controversial call because OU Coach Barry Switzer thought the clock should have run out before the ball was hiked. In the third quarter, the Cowboys led 14-7. OU was ahead 17-14 going into the fourth quarter and OSU had great position with a chance for a go-ahead score. After a fumble, Spencer Tillman scored a 20-yard touchdown for the Sooners and OU won the game 24-14.

The Bedlam game took the rivalry to a new height. Coach Jones said, "It was the only game on national television that day. The whole deal was as big as it could literally get. Even though we didn't win, I thought it almost erased the 'poor Aggie' concept that haunted our fans and our program." [27]

OSU still was ranked number 9 and was invited to play number 7 South Carolina in the Gator Bowl in Jacksonville, Florida. Bob arrived in Florida three days before the game to tape pre-game interviews and send nightly reports back to Channel Four. The game was like a home game for South Carolina because of its proximity to Jacksonville.

OSU scored the first 13 points, then South Carolina went ahead by a point. Scoring on their last drive, the Cowboys won the bowl game 21-14. Thurman Thomas ran for 155 yards and was the Most Valuable Player. Leslie O'Neal and Rod Brown secured their status as All-Americans. It was the first ten-win season in OSU football history. In the final wire service polls, the Cowboys were fifth in the UPI poll and seventh in the AP poll. [28]

CHAPTER NINE

Health Problems

Bob had a way of describing the action on a football field that painted a vivid picture for the fan sitting in his living room in the tiniest town in Oklahoma. The excitement in Bob's voice made the fan part of the OSU family.

—PAT JONES

Dear Santa: The way to make sportscaster Bob Barry happy is for him to beat Linda Cavanaugh just one week at picking football scores.

—JIM LASSITER in *The Daily Oklahoman*

The success of OSU football in 1984 paid at least two dividends—more radio stations wanted to join the Cowboy Sports Network and high school football recruits penciled in OSU on lists of potential colleges. More than 30 radio stations signed on to carry OSU games for the 1985 season.

In the off-season, Bob had spoken with Coach Jones and his staff about the likelihood that *Parade Magazine* All-American and *USA Today* high school offensive player of the year Hart Lee Dykes would sign with the Cowboys. When it was apparent that Dykes would play his college football at OSU, Bob reported the story on Channel Four.

Dykes was a rare find, "a man among boys," according to Coach Jones. The first time Bob met and interviewed Dykes, he could see why the coaching staff was so high on him. He worked hard in practice, was good in the classroom, and was a gifted athlete.[1]

As Bob was preparing for the start of the 1985 season, he had no idea that he would not be in the broadcast booth for the first few games. Since being hospitalized as a child for treatment for injuries suffered in the fall from the second story window of his home and a series of childhood illnesses, Bob had avoided hospitals for nearly 50 years except for a bout with pneumonia. In the summer of 1985, he was 54 years old, relatively healthy, and his career looked bright. He had become a household name at KTVY and was actively recruited to move from Channel Four to KWTV in Oklahoma City.

It was the goal of KWTV general manager Dewayne Harm to have the Oklahoma City market's top-rated news, weather, and sports personalities. KWTV had the top weatherman, Gary England, and Harm recruited the top-rated news anchor, Jack Bowen, from KOCO-TV. Harm approached Bob and said he wanted him at Channel 9 and made Bob a "great" offer which Bob was inclined to accept. Bob discussed the situation with his old friend and boss, Lee Allan Smith, who immediately offered to match the KWTV offer.[2]

Channel Four continued to hold a strong position in the Oklahoma City market, but was challenged by the two other network affiliates, KWTV (CBS) and KOCO (ABC). KTVY General Manager Smith said, "It was not that Channel Four had lessened in quality, but the number and quality of its competitors changed the station's share of the market. Cable television was also beginning to detract viewers from local stations."[3]

Bob felt loyalty to Smith and KTVY. Smith convinced Bob to

consider a new long-time contract with Channel Four that included the payment of lifetime annuities. While Bob and Joan were looking over the contract, an unexpected and near fatal event occurred. On a Sunday afternoon in late August, Bob suffered severe stomach pains that moved into his chest, arms, and shoulder. He called his doctor who immediately sent Bob to Presbyterian Hospital in Oklahoma City.

Shortly after arriving at the hospital, Bob suffered a heart attack. His heart stopped, but hospital attendants were able to revive him and his heart resumed beating. Three of Bob's arteries were clogged, two completely and the other by eighty percent. His physician considered two options—immediate bypass surgery or a much longer regimen of trying to unclog the arteries with medication.[4]

After extensive testing, doctors decided that Bob's best treatment was a quadruple-bypass coronary surgery that was performed on August 29, 1985. The surgery took more than three hours. A hospital spokesman announced Bob's surgery was successful and that he was in critical but stable condition several hours after the bypass.[5]

The night before the surgery, Lee Allan Smith sent KTVY news director Ron Turner to Bob's hospital room to sign his new contract with the television station. Turner told Bob, "Sign this thing and if you die during the operation, the contract with its annuities for Joan go into effect. If you make it through the surgery, you can continue negotiations." Bob remembered, "Lee Allan was being more than a friend, because my wife would have been taken care of if I had died."[6]

Not long after regaining consciousness, Bob began worrying about when he could return to work. Football season was only two weeks away. His doctor told him he would be off work from two to seven weeks. After a week in the hospital, Bob was released to

Joan's care at home. However, he was not released to broadcast OSU's first game. David Garrett filled in as the play-by-play announcer for the first five games of the season.[7]

OSU returned 15 starters in 1985 but had to break in a new quarterback, Ronnie Williams. The first game was at the University of Washington against a Huskies team that had beaten OU in the Orange Bowl the previous year and was picked by *Sports Illustrated* to win the national title. Bob had to listen on the radio from his home as Thurman Thomas ran 40 times for 237 yards as the Cowboys won 31-17. It was a huge win, the second time in two seasons the Cowboys scored impressive opening wins against major national powers. In the post-game show, Coach Jones said Thomas should be a candidate for the Heisman Trophy.[8]

Each week, Thomas piled more yards onto his total rushing effort, although Bob was more impressed by defensive star Leslie O'Neal's monster game against Kansas. O'Neal had eight tackles, two sacks, a forced fumble, a fumble recovery, and an interception against the Jayhawks. By the seventh game of 1985, Thomas had over 1,000 rushing yards. Against Kansas State, Thomas ran for 213 yards and four touchdowns.

OSU lost any chance to win the Big Eight Conference championship with a 15-10 loss to Iowa State, sending the Cowboys season record to 8-2. OSU accepted a bid to play again in the Gator Bowl and then prepared for the annual Bedlam game against OU. Both teams were ranked in the top 20.

Bob was cleared by his doctors to broadcast the 1985 Bedlam contest that was moved to an evening game to accommodate ESPN. At about the time Bob arrived at the stadium with the remainder of the broadcast crew to prepare for the game, a thunderstorm hit. After an hour of lightning and thunder, the temperature plummeted and the liquid turned to sleet, then ice. By game time, the field was a skating rink. The game became known in Bedlam folklore as the Ice Bowl, largely because ESPN announcers Mike Patrick and Paul Maguire called it that for the entire broadcast.

Even with a slick field, Thurman Thomas became the first back that season to run for 100 yards against the OU defense. OU won 13-0 on its way to a national championship. Many fables were born at the Ice Bowl. Bob tells the story about fans after the game sledding down stadium aisles and one lady who supposedly could not make it to the bathroom and was frozen to her seat.

OSU football coach Pat Jones, right, mentored assistant coaches who later became head coaches. Houston Nutt, left, later was head coach at the University of Arkansas and University of Mississippi. Kevin Steele, center was an assistant coach at several major universities and for NFL teams and was head coach at Baylor University for four seasons. *Courtesy OSU Athletic Department.*

Pat Jones remembered, "It was almost like the Twilight Zone. We weren't freezing to death since we were bundled up, but it was surreal because of the lightning and ice and the covered field. Guys were slipping and sliding and trying to scratch footing into the ground." [9]

Coach Pat Jones celebrates with OSU players after the Cowboys beat South Carolina in the Gator Bowl, capping OSU's first ten-win season. *Courtesy OSU Athletic Department.*

KOCO reporter Mick Cornett had decided to leave his seat in the warm press box to experience the game on the sideline. Once during the game, when he looked from the north sideline across the field, the press box looked like "just a glow in the sky" because the air was saturated with fog and sleet.[10]

After the 1985 season, there was much media speculation that OSU coach Jones would leave Stillwater to become head coach at the University of Pittsburgh. Sources at OSU and Pittsburgh theorized it was Jones' job if he wanted it. Jones toyed with the idea for weeks until he made up his mind to remain in Stillwater.

After all the talk about the coach leaving, the Cowboys left for Florida to play Florida State University in the Gator Bowl. One of the highlights of the trip for Bob was a long interview with Florida State coach Bobby Bowden. Thomas had only a mediocre game, with 97 yards rushing, but Hart Lee Dykes set a Gator Bowl record with eight catches for 104 yards. However, OSU's offense could not generate enough points to keep up with the Seminoles who won the game 34-23. Even though the season ended with three losses, it was the first time ever that OSU seniors had played in three consecutive bowl games. To top off the incredible season, Thomas was named first-team All-American.[11]

In January, 1986, Bob was named Oklahoma Sportscaster of the Year for the seventh consecutive season. It was his 14th such honor from the National Association of Sportswriters and Sportscasters.

Winters were tough for Bob because of basketball season. There were twice as many basketball games as football games, and travel often was hazardous in Big Eight Conference play in January and February. Bob said, "It is not easy to get to places like Manhattan, Kansas, and Ames, Iowa, in the best of conditions. Add a wintry mix of ice and snow on the Great Plains, and it becomes a real challenge to arrive at frozen arenas before tipoff."[12]

OSU was usually at home in Stillwater for one game each week with another contest at some distant location. It was difficult for Bob to juggle his home life with his play-by-play assignment and his duties as sports director at Channel Four.

Bob enjoyed his nightly stint at Channel Four. Lee Allan Smith had put together a strong local news presence with Jack Ogle, Ernie Schultz, George Tomek, Brad Edwards, and Linda Cavanaugh. Butch and Ben McCain hosted a morning show. Jim Williams was a popular weatherman.

Cavanaugh, who became the first female co-anchor of the

evening newscasts at Channel Four, was impressed with Bob from the moment she met him as an intern in the newsroom. "He was a giant, both in stature and career," she said. It was obvious to Cavanaugh that Bob was "a gentle man," but was serious about reporting sports. She cited an example, "He firmly believed that sports were supposed to be about the games people played, not the crimes the athletes committed. His philosophy was that if a competitor found his or her name on an arrest warrant, that story belonged in the news, not the sportscast." [13]

When Cavanaugh became a prime time news co-anchor, she and Bob developed a very special on-air chemistry. Bob Barry, Jr., said, "You could tell they were genuine friends and neither had any problem whatsoever with being the butt of jokes or funny comments." [14]

"Bob loves to see people laugh, even if it is at his own expense," Cavanaugh said. Once when Channel Four celebrities went "on the road" to broadcast nightly news shows, they appeared at a luncheon in Ponca City. As part of the visit to the community, each of the news, weather, and sports anchors "said a few words." When the master of ceremonies introduced Bob, he just stayed in his seat fumbling with his napkin instead of heading for the podium. After a long silence, Bob approached the microphone and apologized. His zipper had broken and he was tucking a napkin in his belt. An older lady, seated in the back of the room, tried to make Bob more comfortable and yelled, "It's no big deal!" Bob blushed and said, "Well, that may be true, but you don't have to tell everyone." [15]

A popular segment for viewers was Bob's challenge to Cavanaugh to make weekly predictions during football season. Cavanaugh knew very little about football, but "in a weak moment," agreed to the on-the-air predictions. "Bob thought I would be an easy mark," she remembered, "which he had every reason to believe. But, what he did not count on was blind luck." [16]

On Wednesdays, Bob would hand Cavanaugh a list of ten college games from which to pick a winner. She took a pen and randomly circled the teams she thought would win. On the other hand, Bob studied the sheet and analyzed injuries, player matchups, and point spreads. "After the first few weeks, when I guessed 70 percent of the winners and Bob barely managed 50 percent, the tradition was born that lasted a good 15 years," she said. [17]

Linda Cavanaugh, left, and Bob with the San Diego Chicken in the Channel Four studios in the early 1980s. The chicken helped Cavanaugh and Bob make weekly football predictions. *Courtesy KFOR-TV.*

One week, Cavanaugh slipped below her average and Bob suggested that a monkey might give her "a little help to raise her average." Cavanaugh's own premise was that a monkey could do better at predicting the outcome of college football games than Bob. Cavanaugh called the Oklahoma City zoo to see if Channel Four could borrow a monkey for the prediction segment. Zoo officials said, "no," but they did have a gorilla. "Even better!" she remembered. A baby female gorilla was brought to the television station and placed on the set while Cavanaugh and Bob taped the predictions for the week. The gorilla's handlers warned the two broadcasters to watch out for their thumbs. Gorillas were known to attack an opponent's thumbs in a fight to disable them.[18]

"We no sooner started than that little gorilla took one look at Bob and sunk her teeth into Bob's thumb," Cavanaugh said. The handlers were "beside themselves," yelling "We've got to get a tetanus shot!" Bob was trying to stop the bleeding and asked, "Where do I go to get a tetanus shot?" The zookeepers replied, "Not you! We need to get a tetanus shot for the gorilla." Cavanaugh remembered, "It was the first time I ever saw Bob with a loss for words and the last time we had a live animal on the football prediction show." [19]

KTVY spent a lot of effort and money getting their personalities live before viewers around the state, In 1986, Channel Four broadcast its news shows at 5:00 p.m., 6:00 p.m., and 10:00 p.m. from six cities across the state during a very hectic week. A 35-person crew was required to make certain all the microphones worked, the electrical hookups were solid, and the pictures were perfect. The road crew operated from a 40-foot remote production truck. [20]

Bob, Jane Jayroe, Jerry Adams, Linda Cavanaugh, and Jim Williams broadcast their evening segments from Shawnee, Purcell, Duncan, El Reno, Enid, and Woodward. *PM Magazine* also was broadcast live each night from the towns. KTVY General Manager Bob Finke said, "Meeting the people, our viewers, is important to us." Finke wanted Channel Four to "get the station's presence felt around the state." [21]

When Jayroe, a former Miss America, came to Channel Four in 1984 after successful years as a news anchor at KOCO-TV in Oklahoma City and in the Dallas-Fort Worth market, she had difficulty convincing everyone in the Channel Four newsroom she was a hard-working journalist and not "just a former Miss America." "It was as cold as a deep freeze," she remembered, "until Bob and Linda Cavanaugh thawed the cold in my work environment. Bob was just Bob—friendly, funny, nice guy to everyone, including me as a newcomer. His kindness melted a lot of emotional ice." [22]

Jayroe appreciated Bob's humor and his professionalism. She said, "He set a higher standard. Because of the pressure of time in a newscast, many folks grow horns. You can see them across the busy newsroom as they sweat while writing their copy. Their foreheads are wrinkled, and if someone says something to them at the wrong time, they explode." Jayroe says Bob "created a different culture for behavior." He could hurry with the best and experienced anxiety, but "when things didn't go well he never took out his frustrations out on some undeserving soul." [23]

As the 1986 football season loomed on the horizon, Bob joined OSU players, coaches, cheerleaders, and the Cowboy band at a Cowboy Football Preview and Barbecue at Will Rogers Park in northwest Oklahoma City. Coach Jones, his coaching staff, athletic director Myron Roderick, and leading players addressed the crowd. Bob was the master of ceremonies for a huge crowd at the event sponsored by the OSU Alumni Association.

CHAPTER TEN

Becoming a Legend

I learned a lot about life from Bob in three decades in the same newsroom.

—LINDA CAVANAUGH

In the 1980s, Bob was around some of the greatest athletes of all time—and they all trusted him. They were the premier people in the country and they respected Bob and were glad to know him.

—PAT JONES

Bob and other sportscasters and sportswriters were enthralled with the recruiting of high school football prospects in 1986. Because Bob was the voice of the OSU Cowboys, he was especially interested in Coach Pat Jones and his staff recruiting Midwest City High School quarterback Mike Gundy.

Most Midwest City players leaned toward playing for OU which had played in three straight bowl games and was winning big. However, Jones and his assistant coaches told Gundy that OU was not going to scrap the wishbone formation to accommodate him as a throwing quarterback. Gundy was a "bit undersized," but OSU wanted him badly. He was named the state's player of the year and ultimately finished his career at OSU as the leading passer in Big Eight Conference history. He later became the head football coach at OSU.[1]

After newspapers reported that Gundy was going to commit to OU, Coach Jones called him and asked him about the report. Gundy said, "Don't worry about it, Coach." Soon, Gundy announced his intention to attend OSU.[2] Gundy knew Bob's reputation as the longtime voice of the Sooners and now the voice of OSU football. Gundy remembered, "The first time I did an interview with him, he was so gracious and had a smile on his face. He always was in a good mood. You could hear his distinctive laugh across a crowded room. He was such a pleasure to be around."[3]

The OSU recruiting class of 1986 was unbelievably talented. In addition to Gundy, who ultimately became the Cowboys' all-time leading passer and successful head coach, Gerald Hudson led the NCAA in rushing in his senior season and the class included a little-known running back, Barry Sanders, from Wichita North High School in Kansas. OSU assistant coach George Walstad was responsible for recruiting in Kansas and discovered Sanders who was being pursued only by Iowa State University and the University of Tulsa. For some reason, neither of the Big Eight schools in his home state, Kansas or Kansas State, showed any interest in Sanders.[4]

OSU was loaded with running backs. Thurman Thomas was a returning starter, had finished tenth in the Heisman Trophy balloting the year before as a sophomore, and was poised to make a sincere effort to win the Heisman. However, in February, 1986, Thomas injured his knee playing basketball and underwent surgery.

Bob, Tom Dirato, and the broadcast crew headed for Lafayette in southern Louisiana for the first game of the OSU football season in early September. It was an interesting trip. The football field for the University of Southwestern Louisiana was adjacent to a swamp that contained alligators and turtles. Cajun Field almost was a trap for the Cowboys that day. Led by future NFL star Brian Mitchell, Southwestern Louisiana scored with three minutes to go in the game to go up 20-9. However, Bobby Riley scored on a 97-yard kickoff return and, after a defensive stop, Ronnie Williams threw an 11-yard pass to Hart Lee Dykes with eight seconds left for a 21-20 Cowboys win.[5]

On the way back to Stillwater on the team airplane, Coach Jones referred to Bob's heart attack the previous year on the intercom. Jones said, "What a close game, winning it in the final eight seconds. If that didn't give Bob Barry another heart attack, nothing will!"[6]

Bob had an "unbelievable" working relationship with the OSU coaching staff. Coach Jones said, "Bob was very popular with the coaches and their staff because he treated everyone fairly." Jones also recognized that Bob was not just "putting on a show" at a coaches meeting or post-game meal. He remembered once playing golf with Bob and Jimmy Johnson at the Oklahoma City Golf and Country Club. Jones said, "I couldn't help but notice how friendly Bob was to everyone. Everybody knew him and liked him."[7]

After a disappointing loss to Tulsa, Coach Jones said he might consider a quarterback change should Williams continue to throw interceptions. He had thrown four interceptions in two games. In the third game of the season against Houston, Williams threw another interception in the first half and the Cowboys trailed 21-3 at halftime. Jones had seen enough. He decided to turn to his No. 3 quarterback, true freshman, Mike Gundy. The change could have sparked controversy on the team, especially with leading players such as Thurman Thomas and Hart Lee Dykes who had loyalty to Williams. But Williams was moved to wide receiver, had a reasonably good attitude about the change, and major problems were averted.[8]

OSU beat Illinois State in Gundy's first start at quarterback and Barry Sanders carried the ball for more than 100 yards for the first time in his collegiate career. The Cowboys lost to third-ranked Nebraska and fifth-ranked OU in successive weeks. In the post-game show after the game against the Sooners, Coach Jones said he had never been prouder of a team. OU was leading the nation in rushing, yet OSU did not give up an offensive touchdown. The Sooners won 19-0 on an interception return and four field goals.[9]

Quarterback Mike Gundy of Midwest City, Oklahoma, was later an assistant coach and head football coach at OSU. Gundy said about Bob, "He is a genuine person and will always be remembered for trying to find the good in any athlete or coach even during disastrous seasons." *Courtesy OSU Athletic Department.*

A newspaper advertisement in 1987 promoted Bob's play-by-play broadcast of OSU football on WKY-Radio in Oklahoma City, the flagship station of the Cowboys Sports Network. *Courtesy Oklahoma Publishing Company.*

Bob, second from right, loved golf tournaments. At Oak Tree Country Club, he played in a group with professional golf star Lee Trevino, third from left, and Oak Tree members in a 1980's tournament.

The Cowboys swept their last three games against Kansas State, Iowa State, and Missouri as Gundy began having success, completing 11 passes to Hart Lee Dykes against Iowa State. Jones later said 1986 may have been his best coaching job. Bob could see that OSU's young players now had a lot of confidence and that the next two years might be very special. He was right.[10]

For the 1987 basketball campaign, Gallagher Hall, originally named for legendary OSU wrestling coach Ed Gallagher, underwent major renovations and was renamed Gallagher-Iba Arena, as a tribute to Gallagher and long-time basketball coach and athletic director Henry Iba. Bob was master of ceremonies for the ceremony dedicating the renovated facility. Leonard Hamilton, a North Carolina native and an assistant coach at the University of Kentucky, had

Bob interviews former OU, UCLA, and Dallas Cowboys quarterback Troy Aikman during halftime of an OU basketball game.

A perk of the sportscasting business is getting to meet and interview sports celebrities such as Hall of Fame quarterback, Joe Namath, left.

Bob interviews former NFL and Southern Methodist University quarterback Don Meredith who became "Dandy Don" Meredith in the early days of ABC-TV's Monday Night Football.

replaced Paul Hansen as OSU basketball coach the year before.

Before the 1987 football season, Coach Jones prophetically talked about OSU's return game. In the first game of the season, Barry Sanders returned the opening kickoff 100 yards for a touchdown as OSU beat Tulsa in a shootout, 39-28. Thurman Thomas ran for 164 yards. Jones knew his offensive team was special, but could not have known that it contained two future members of the

National Football League Hall of Fame, Thomas and Sanders.

When Bob arrived in Laramie, Wyoming, for OSU's game against the University of Wyoming, the sign at the Holiday Inn said, "Welcome, University of Oklahoma." Athletic Director Myron Roderick was mad and made the hotel management change the sign within the hour. The Cowboys beat Wyoming in a game in which Thomas ran for 193 yards and Gundy threw for 325 yards.

After a win against Colorado, OSU was 5-0 for the first time since 1945 and the Cowboys were ranked No. 12 in the Associated Press poll. Unfortunately, OSU met second-ranked Nebraska the following week in Stillwater and lost 35-0. OSU beat sixth-ranked Missouri 24-20 when Gundy threw a touchdown pass to J.R. Dillard in the fourth quarter. Thomas and Sanders both rushed for more than 100 yards in a Halloween homecoming game against Kansas State. The Cowboys won 56-7. Jones began rotating Thomas and Sanders. Thomas played the first three series, Sanders the next three series, and alternated for the remainder of the game. Jones said, "It was a great arrangement." [11]

Bob liked Coach Jones and enjoyed their relaxed relationship. Bob knew Jones had a great mind for coaching, but was more impressed with his big heart and ability to relate with players on a very common level. In a loss against OU, Sooner quarterback Jamelle Holieway severely injured his knee on a play right in front of the OSU bench. Coach Jones immediately ran out onto the field and grabbed Holieway and made him lie down slowly as the coach yelled for OU trainer, Dan Pickett. Bob said, "Not every coach would have cared about another team's player. But at that moment, it was all about a kid who was hurt. It did not matter that it was in the middle of Bedlam." [12]

Thomas became OSU's career rushing leader when he ran for 293 yards against Iowa State in the Cowboys' final regular season game. It was a game for several records. Gundy set single-season records for passing yardage and touchdowns. Dykes became the Cowboys' career leader in receiving yards.

Bob had to be away from home on Christmas Day as OSU accepted a bid to play in the Sun Bowl in El Paso, Texas, against the University of West Virginia. The Cowboys, behind Thomas' 157 yards, beat West Virginia 35-33. It was the second ten-win season for OSU in four years. The Cowboys ended the season ranked No. 11.

Coach Jones wrote a book with sportswriter Jimmie Trammel, *Tales From Oklahoma State Football*, in which he titled the chapter

Famed sportscaster Curt Gowdy, left, joins Bob on the set of WKY-TV. In high school, Bob listened to Gowdy broadcast Oklahoma City Indians baseball and OU football games.

Thurman Thomas overshadowed Barry Sanders in the Cowboys backfield in 1987. After college, Thomas had an outstanding NFL career with Buffalo and Miami. He is a member of the Pro Football Hall of Fame. *Courtesy Buffalo Bills.*

about the 1988 season "Run to the Heisman." It was one of the most spectacular years in college football history and, according to Jones, was "a milestone in Oklahoma State's football history."[13]

Everywhere Bob went, he was asked by Cowboys fans, "How will OSU replace Thurman Thomas?" The answer was Barry Sanders. Coach Jones said, "We've got a young man who was an All-American kick returner and we think he will be OK at tailback." Mick Cornett remembered, "It was not surprising that Sanders would become a worthy replacement for Thomas because of OSU returning a veteran offensive line that could plow huge holes in the opponent's front line."[14]

The result was one of the best offenses in the history of college football. OSU led the nation in scoring with 47.5 points per game and was second to the University of Utah in total yards. Sanders ran for 2,628 yards and scored 39 touchdowns—the most productive season for a running back in college football history.[15]

The Cowboys beat Miami of Ohio 52-20 in the season opener. Sanders, for the second season in a row, ran the opening kickoff back for a touchdown, a feat never duplicated in NCAA history. Gundy became OSU's all-time passing leader even though he was playing only in the first game of his junior season. In the second game, a night affair in Stillwater, Sanders ran for 58 yards and a touchdown on the third play of the game. OSU beat Texas A & M 52-15.

OSU was ranked No. 13 when the Cowboys played Tulsa. The nation's sports media began talking about Sanders as a potential Heisman Trophy candidate. The young man from Wichita did not disappoint Cowboy faithful when he ran for a school-record 304 yards and scored five touchdowns in a huge win over the Golden Hurricane. OSU Sports Information Director Steve Buzzard began sending mail-outs to sportswriters and other media outlets in the country, letting them know about Sanders' accomplishments.

It was cold in early November when Bob flew on a chartered prop engine plane to Lincoln, Nebraska, for the annual showdown with the Cornhuskers. OSU was ranked No. 10 and Nebraska was No. 7. On the plane with Bob were Robert Allen and Van Shea Iven. The Cowboys were 4-0 and Sanders had rushed for more than 800 yards. With Gundy, Dykes, and the "War Pigs" offensive line, many Cowboys were convinced OSU would break a 28-year drought and beat Nebraska for the first time since 1961.[16]

Allen, a Channel Four sports reporter, and later a member of the Cowboys Sports Radio Network, remembered:

What we saw was a nightmare as the Cowboys turned the ball over several times early, including a Mike Gundy interception thrown deep in Nebraska territory as OSU was driving to try to tie the game at 7-7. Instead of an OSU touchdown, the pick was returned for a score by the Huskers. The Cowboys defense was absolutely outmanned. By early in the second quarter, Nebraska had taken a 42-0 lead.[17]

Even though OSU eventually lost 63-42, the Cowboys' 42 points was the most ever scored against a Tom Osborne-coached team and the most points scored by a Nebraska opponent in Lincoln in 40 years. Sanders made the otherwise tragic day a little more bearable with 189 yards in rushing.

In the game against Kansas State, Sanders rushed for 320 yards, the first back in NCAA history to have two 300-yard games in a season. In the Bedlam game, OSU led 28-24 with 8:45 left in the game, but because of a dropped pass and critical penalty, ultimately lost to OU 31-28. OU's Mike Gaddis and Sanders both rushed for more than 200 yards. Sanders' 215 yards was the second best game ever against a Sooner defense. The performance moved Sanders ahead of Oklahoma native Troy Aikman of UCLA in the Scripps-Howard Heisman Trophy poll.

The regular season finale in 1988 against Texas Tech was played in Tokyo, Japan. Immediately, there was a conflict because the Heisman Trophy announcement was scheduled for the same day OSU was a half-world away. Sanders had been invited to New York for the trophy presentation along with Aikman, Rodney Peete of the University of Southern California, Major Harris of West Virginia University, and Steve Walsh of Miami of Florida.

Bob joined OSU officials on a bus ride to Dallas to catch a Boeing 747 that carried the Cowboys, Red Raiders, the Grambling University band, and the Miami Dolphin cheerleaders. However, Bob's color man, Dirato, could not make the trip. Assistant OSU athletic director Dave Martin was tabbed to do color for the radio broadcast for the first time in his life and former OSU President Lawrence Boger kept statistics for Bob, who bragged, "It was the first broadcast ever where the stats man was a president emeritus of a university." [18]

The site of the game in Japan was the Tokyo Dome which was primarily used for baseball. There was no press box so Bob and Texas Tech broadcaster Jack Dale talked a stadium official, through an interpreter, into rigging up a temporary press box in what would have been the left field bleachers of the stadium. There was no scoreboard in sight, so during the game, Bob had to look behind him to see the clock and other information displayed on the scoreboard.

OU's athletic director, Donnie Duncan, was present for the festivities because OU was preparing to play a game in Japan the following year. When Duncan was introduced at a banquet as "Donnie Duncan of Oklahoma State," the OSU crowd roared with laughter.

The night before the game, Bob stayed late at the Tokyo Dome to oversee installation of the telephone line that would carry the game back to Oklahoma on the radio stations on the Cowboy Radio Network. Realizing he was by himself, Bob tried to hail a taxi outside the stadium. With a huge language barrier between Bob and the taxi driver, Bob ended up at the wrong hotel. He worried that Joan would think he had been killed or kidnapped in a strange land. Finally, Bob arrived safely at his hotel and prepared for the next day's game.[19]

However, before the game, the Heisman Trophy announcement was being made in New York City at about 2:00 a.m. Tokyo time. Sanders' parents and brother were appearing on his behalf at the awards ceremony at the Downtown Athletic Club. Sanders had to be coerced by Coach Jones to get up in the wee hours of the morning and be driven to a television studio owned by CBS in downtown Tokyo. When it was announced that Sanders was the winner, he made a few brief comments and then was whisked away without an

Barry Sanders won the Heisman Trophy in 1988 when he established 34 NCAA records and posted the best rushing season in college football history. *Courtesy OSU Athletic Department.*

interview. Jones' reasoning was that his star running back was due to play football in a game that kicked off in less than seven hours.

With his scaled-down broadcast team, Bob was his own engineer for the game. He set up the equipment and got ready to take the air. He opened the broadcast, "Hello everyone, Bob Barry speaking to you from the Tokyo Dome in Tokyo, Japan, ready for the OSU-Texas Tech game. With me is Dave Martin." Martin said, "Well, Tom." Bob said, "No Dave, I'm not Tom, I'm Bob." Martin was petrified.[20]

It was the most unusual circumstances under which Bob ever called a game. There were problems from the beginning. Bob called it his "roughest game" ever:

We were so low, about nine rows up, I couldn't tell whether the ball was on the eight or 18-yard-line. Barry Sanders was about to break the NCAA rushing record so President Boger was keeping track of it. ESPN was monitoring our broadcast so they could report on the record-breaking performance. Once President Boger said on the intercom, "He's broken the record," and I announced the record-breaking run to the world. Then Boger quickly said, "No, I added wrong!" I had to correct the error.[21]

The public address announcements were in Japanese, no help to Bob in trying to figure out when Sanders broke the rushing record. It was a shootout with OSU winning 45-42. Texas Tech quarterback Billy Joe Tolliver led the Southwest Conference in passing that season and OSU had a difficult time stopping him. He threw for a school-record 446 yards. Coach Jones later wrote:

> *The Japanese crowd didn't understand the game, but they had been given noisemakers and little drums and everything. Every time somebody threw the ball, they cheered, whether it was completed or not, so you can imagine how many times they cheered considering the number of passes Tolliver fired. There were no acoustics in the building. It was incredibly noisy and the Grambling band was right there next to our bench. Because of the loudness quotient, my head was splitting.[22]*

The week after the Cowboys arrived home to Stillwater, Coach Jones accompanied Sanders to New York City for a banquet to honor the new Heisman Trophy winner. Sportscaster Mick Cornett was at the banquet and watched Sanders, "a very mild-mannered and bashful young man," finally recognize the significance of winning the most prestigious award in college football. The importance of winning the Heisman may have hit Sanders when former Heisman winner and University of Texas running back Earl Campbell asked for Sanders autograph.[23]

OSU accepted a bid to play in the Holiday Bowl in San Diego, California. The opponent was Wyoming which was destroyed by OSU in Jack Murphy Stadium, ironically named for a Tulsa, Oklahoma native who had gone west and became San Diego's premier sportswriter for 30 years before the new stadium was named for him after his death in 1980. OSU won 62-14, the Cowboys' tenth win of the season, and the Heisman Trophy winner, Sanders, ran wild. All OSU fans were hoping that he would return for his senior season.

However, shortly after the game Sanders' father, William Sanders, was waiting for Coach Jones beside one of the pillars outside the dressing room. The elder Sanders told the coach that his son was ready to leave school a year early and enter the NFL draft.[24]

OSU went from the mountain top of football to the valley of despair within a month. In January, 1989, the NCAA placed the Cowboys on a four-year probation for recruiting violations, largely surrounding the recruitment of Hart Lee Dykes. The sanctions were severe—no bowl games for three years, a two-year ban on television, and a loss of 15 scholarships over a three-year period. The Cowboys went from ten-win seasons to ten-loss seasons.

But after football, there always was basketball to cover through the winter months. Bob faithfully provided OSU fans with a vivid description of Cowboys basketball fortunes, including play in the Big Eight tournament in Kansas City each spring.

After calling a game at Kemper Arena, Bob intended to find his rental car and head for the hotel to rest until it was time to go on the air again. However, he forgot where he parked the vehicle and what color it was.

Bob was the prime time sports anchor at Channel Four for two generations of Oklahoma sports fans.

Bob with Oklahoma native and Baseball Hall of Fame catcher Johnny Bench when Bench was inducted into the Oklahoma Sports Hall of Fame.

He walked around the parking lot in the cold for what seemed like an eternity, but realized he would never find the car. Linda Cavanaugh, who has told the story to audiences and Bob's fans for years, said, "Even though Bob says he was in the parking lot the whole time, I believe he went back into the arena and bought two hot dogs and watched the next game. He was in hog heaven! He had junk food at his fingertips and a great game in front of him." [25]

Bob's version of the event is that he waited for the game to end and for Kemper Arena to clear. Even though he was freezing and his wife, Joan, and camera man Oliver Murray thought he had been kidnapped, he ultimately found the rental car by process of elimination. When all the fans left, the rental car was the only vehicle left in the massive parking lot. [26]

By 1990, college football and basketball had become big business. OSU Regents approved a three-year contract with Clear Channel Communications to broadcast OSU football and basketball games. The contract provided OSU with $675,000 annually, four times more than the previous contract with Learfield Communications. Clear Channel also owned the broadcast rights to OU football and baseball contests. OSU officials announced that Bob would remain the play-by-play announcer and Tom Dirato would continue to serve as color commentator. [27]

A change for Bob was the hiring of Eddie Sutton as the new head basketball coach to replace Leonard Hamilton who had accepted the head coaching job at the University of Miami, Florida. Hamilton coached the Hurricanes for a decade, was head coach of the NBA Washington Wizards for one season, and is now head basketball coach at Florida State University.

Sutton, who played basketball for the Cowboys for Coach Henry Iba, had a successful coaching record at Creighton University, the University of Arkansas, and the University of Kentucky. He later had the rare distinction of taking two schools, Arkansas and OSU, to the Final Four and was the first coach in NCAA history to lead four schools to the NCAA Tournament.

There was no doubt Sutton was brought to Stillwater to restore the honor and tradition of Cowboy basketball that previously had

been largely dormant. Bob visited Sutton who was humble about his selection to lead his old school. From the very beginning of their relationship, Bob believed that Sutton was "a great basketball mind" and

Eddie Sutton became men's basketball coach at OSU in 1990, Bob's final season as the "Voice of the Cowboys." *Courtesy OSU Athletic Department.*

that OSU officials had picked the one coach who could turn the basketball program at OSU around. OSU had made post-season appearances only three times since joining the Big Eight Conference in 1957.[28]

Sutton proved his supporters right. He led the Cowboys to a first-place finish in the Big Eight Conference tournament, a 24-8 season record, and a trip to the Sweet Sixteen of the NCAA Tournament, the first invitation to the "Big Dance" since 1983. Later, in 1995, OSU, under the leadership of Bryant "Big Country" Reeves and Randy Rutherford, made it to the Final Four of the NCAA Tournament.

CHAPTER ELEVEN

Voice of the Sooners...Again

*Being the respected voice of OU and OSU for a lifetime has
set the bar very high for future aspiring sports personalities.*

—DEE SADLER

There was another name change for Channel Four in 1990.
The Gannett Company had purchased KTVY's owner, the Evening
News Association, in 1986. Because Gannett also owned KOCO-
TV in Oklahoma City, the Federal Communications Commission
required the company to sell one of the television stations. Knight
Ridder bought Channel Four and in 1989 sold the station to Palmer
Communications which changed the call letters to KFOR-TV.

Also in 1990, Bob completed 18 years of broadcasting OSU
football games. However, he began sensing that new OSU athletic
director James Garner, who replaced the retiring Myron Roderick,
might prefer someone else to be the voice of OSU football and basketball. Garner was great friends with KWTV sports director Bill
Teegins. Bob sometimes heard rumors that Garner would like to
bring Teegins to Stillwater to broadcast Cowboy sports. However,
Garner never said a disparaging word to Bob.[1]

The first sign that John Brooks might not continue to be the
voice of the Sooners in 1991 came in November, 1990, when the

American Network Group, Inc. purchased the rights to broadcast
OU football and basketball games for three years. Brooks, who
had broadcast OU football games for 13 years as the play-by-play
announcer, was never contacted by the new group. Instead, Brooks
signed a three-year contract with Clear Channel Communications,
the previous OU broadcast-rights owner, which also owned KTOK
Radio, the Sooner Network flagship station in Oklahoma City. Clear
Channel also had won the bid for the broadcast rights for OSU football and basketball for the 1991 seasons. Brooks told Bob Hersom
at *The Daily Oklahoman*, "Barring an unforeseen miracle, I will not
be back at OU." [2]

Publicly, no one seriously believed Bob would leave his post as
the voice of the Cowboys. When Brooks was asked where he might
land as the play-by-play announcer, he immediately ruled out OSU,
saying, "I don't think it takes a mental giant to realize that certainly
Oklahoma State wouldn't be considered. Obviously they're not going to change from Bob Barry." [3]

Privately, Bob learned from good friends in Norman that
Brooks had "fallen out of favor" with OU athletic director Donnie
Duncan. Just before Christmas, 1990, Duncan called Bob and said,
"If you can get out of your contract at OSU, we'd like to have you
back in Norman." Even though Bob was perfectly happy with the
way he had been treated for nearly two decades as a member of
the OSU family, he and Joan talked into the night about how much
easier it would be for Bob to broadcast OU games with Owen Field
and the Lloyd Noble Center just a few miles from their Norman
home. Joan openly had been concerned for years about Bob driving to Stillwater 20 times a year for football and basketball games,
especially coming home late at night after basketball games. [4]

Friends envied the close relationship between Bob and Joan. Here they dance while preparing Thanksgiving dinner in the Barry kitchen.

In addition, the "changing of the guard" at OSU caused Bob to think hard about returning to OU. His dear friends, athletic director Myron Roderick and OSU President Lawrence Boger, had retired. Admittedly, Bob did not have as close relations with their successors. After he talked the situation over with Joan, Bob called Duncan back and said, "I'm interested in coming back to OU!"[5]

In January, 1991, Bob approached OSU athletic director Garner and told him he would like to return to OU as the play-by-play announcer. Garner's concern was that OSU would look bad if the public thought Bob was being recruited by OU. Bob assured Garner that he would never do anything to hurt OSU's image. Finally, Bob told Garner, "Because I am under contract with OSU, you can legally keep me from doing OU games, but I am not doing OSU games. I don't mean to be rude, but my mind is made up." After several sessions with Garner and OSU legal counsel throughout the spring, Bob was released from his contract with OSU in May. Part of the consideration was that KFOR-TV run OSU public service announcements in lieu of a buyout of Bob's contract with the university.[6]

Like most big sports news in Oklahoma, the story that Bob might again be the voice of the Sooners leaked out. Callers to radio talk shows and letters to the editor of the state's newspapers expressed varying opinions. Many oldtimers were excited about Bob returning to the microphone for OU sports. OSU fans who had become accustomed to his description of Cowboy football and basketball were sad that he might leave.

Not everyone was excited about the possibility of Bob returning to the play-by-play job that he had begun in 1961 in Norman. An OU fan from Seminole wrote a letter to the editor of *The Daily Oklahoman* saying that even though he had revered Bob and Jack Ogle doing OU games in past decades, Bob had made too many comments to "blemish" OU sports. The writer said, "I cannot forget some of those comments, for they cut to the bone." The OU fan called Bob "Agent Orange" and suggested that OU officials reconsider any consideration of Bob to return as the voice of the Sooners.[7]

By May, 1991, there were still no decisions made as who would broadcast either OU, OSU, or University of Tulsa football and basketball games. The uncertainty left sports columnist John Rohde to comment, "I don't know what's going to happen, but I do know it's a mess." It was speculated that Bob, Bob Barry, Jr., John Brooks, Tom Dirato, David Garrett, Mike Treps, John Walls, Robbie Robertson, Bill Teegins, and Kevin Ward all were candidates for varying positions in the broadcast crews for the three schools. Bob told *The Daily Oklahoman*, "I never in my wildest imagination ever thought something like this would ever occur and I am very fortunate to be in a position to make a decision."[8]

Rohde predicted that the OU football broadcast team would be Bob, Treps, and Robertson, OU basketball broadcasters would be Bob and Ward or Bob Barry, Jr., OSU football games would be broadcast by Garrett, Teegins, and Dirato, OSU basketball would be called by Garrett and Dirato, and TU football would be broadcast by Brooks and perhaps former TU and Seattle Seahawks wide receiver Steve Largent.[9]

Behind the scenes, Bob was guaranteed he would become voice of the Sooners again, but he could not publicly discuss the situation for several weeks. Meanwhile, Teegins was contacted by OSU officials who recognized his popularity in the Oklahoma City market. Teegins shared his enthusiasm with KWTV news anchor Ed Murray, who remembered, "Bill wanted the job real bad and wanted to quickly bone up on radio play-by-play just in case." Murray found in the Channel Nine files old play-by-play sheets from the previous OSU season. The sheets described everything that happened in a particular game, from the coin flip and wind direction, to the individual players involved in a play.[10]

Using the play-by-play sheets, Teegins went into a sound booth and created a play-by-play audition tape that he sent to OSU.

Bob, right, and former Oklahoma State Banking Commissioner Robert Empie talk at a reunion of Classen High School graduates.

Within a short time, OSU told Teegins he had the job, but, like Bob, could not talk about it until both universities coordinated the release of the information.[11]

On July 21, Bob was announced as the new voice of the Sooners with OU sports information director Mike Treps as the color commentator and Mark Mathew as the sideline reporter. Michael Dean, who worked at KOMA Radio, the new flagship station of the Sooner Sports Network, became producer-engineer of the broadcasts. Treps had been play-by-play announcer for OU football games for four years and served as color commentator for Brooks for 12 seasons. Mathew, who broadcast football and basketball games for Iowa State University where Duncan had been athletic director, was hired by KOMA Radio. Mathew was tabbed to provide daily reports during football and basketball seasons on the progress of Sooner teams. For the first time in decades, WKY Radio did not broadcast either OU or OSU football and basketball games.

American Network Group vice president Tom Stevens told reporters, "Barry and Treps give us a tandem that is second to none in college football." Bob said, "I have been honored to call games for both state universities. Being part of OSU sports has been special, but to come back to my alma mater is a very happy experience for me indeed."[12]

OSU's Garner was classy in his response to the announcement: *I understand and appreciate Bob's decision to make a change. I believe he is doing it for all the right reasons. Bob has meant a lot to the Cowboy family for the past two decades and he will always have a place in OSU's football and basketball history. We wish him the best.*[13]

Teegins officially was announced as the play-by-play announcer for the Cowboys with John Walls, sports director at KOTV-TV in Tulsa, as color commentator, and Dirato, director of radio and television for OSU's athletic department, as sideline reporter and host of the locker room show and the coach's weekly show. KTOK sports director David Garrett was hired to host a 30-minute pre-game show and Kevin Ward was host of a scoreboard show following each football game on the Cowboy Network.[14]

Immediately, sportswriters began to weigh in on the new broadcast team at OU. Bob Hersom wrote in *The Daily Oklahoman*, "Barry and Treps have been less than best buddies for several years. But both men are professionals, and the personal situation should not be a professional problem." Hersom also predicted Bob would have a less than smooth return to Norman:

Barry faces the toughest transition. Though he was OU's play-by-play voice for 13 seasons, he has been the voice of OSU the past 18 years. And Barry is succeeding one of the best in the business, John Brooks, OU's play-by-play voice for 13 years in football and 16 years in basketball.[15]

Again, the switchboards at sports call-in shows lit up and sports editors received a lot of mail discussing Bob's return to OU. Some fans praised Bob, others suggested that OU fans should boycott his broadcasts. P.E. Chapman of Norman wondered why all the fuss. He wrote:

After all, I can't think of one announcer who fumbled inside the 5 against Texas or made the game-deciding play against Nebraska in the fourth quarter. The radio broadcast crew is an extension of the team and for many fans is their only link to the game. This is especially true for out-of-state fans, handi-capped individuals, during TV blackout or probation games, or

*those road games too distant to attend. Many fans just like to
listen to the radio at the game because it adds to their under-
standing of the game or perhaps they gain insight into strategy
or information about key injuries.*[16]

The OU fan also served as a balancing act between letters for and
against Bob. Chapman said, "Regardless of where one's loyalties may
lie, Bob Barry is a true professional and I somehow feel he will do
a fine job as voice of the Sooners during his second stint as play-by-
play announcer." [17]

Shortly after he was announced as the new voice of the Sooners, Bob called Terry McLemore who had served as statistician on
OU football broadcasts with John Brooks since 1986. Bob's friends
at OU said McLemore had done a terrific job. When Bob invited
McLemore to continue to provide instant statistics for the radio broadcast, McLemore accepted. He said, "I had been close to Brooks and
thought I might not be able to stay on. However, when Bob graciously
asked me to stay, I jumped at the opportunity and have loved every
minute of it." [18]

In the 18 years Bob had been officially gone from OU sports, he
saw the football team in person just once each season when the Sooners played OSU and broadcast at least two OU-OSU basketball games
each season. He had missed the entire Barry Switzer Era at OU, three
national championships, and Billy Sims winning the Heisman Trophy
in 1978. Even though Switzer was unable to match Bud Wilkinson's
unimaginable string of 13 consecutive conference championships, he
did win 12 conference crowns himself during his 16-year head coaching career at OU that ended with the 1988 season. He was 8-5 in bowl
games. Switzer later was coach of the Dallas Cowboys and won Super
Bowl XXX and was inducted into the College Football Hall of Fame.

In 1989, OU was placed on probation by the NCAA for rules violations. The Sooners were not allowed to appear on television or play in bowl games for two years and scholarships were drastically cut. When Switzer resigned, he was replaced by Gary Gibbs, OU's defensive coordinator. Gibbs was in his third year as head coach when Bob resumed his post high above Owen Field in the newly-refurbished press box as voice of the Sooners.

Gibbs was a solid linebacker at OU from 1972 to 1974 and, after graduation, spent the next several years as an assistant coach and was promoted to defensive coordinator in 1981. In his first two years, Gibbs tried to field a team short on scholarships and unable to be seen on television. He posted a 7-4 record in 1989 and tied for second place in the Big Eight Conference in 1990.

In Bob's first season back as the voice of the Sooners, Gibbs' team went 9-3, finished third in the Big Eight, and beat the University of Virginia in the Gator Bowl 48-14.

During the 1991 season, *The Daily Oklahoman* featured Bob in a "Wednesday's Witness" column written by sportswriter Mike Baldwin. Bob explained that him getting the OU job was never "me versus Brooks." Bob always understood that Brooks already was out of the picture before he ever was contacted about becoming the play-by-play announcer for the Sooners a second time.[19]

In the special feature, Bob was allowed to explain what a thrill it was for him to be back at OU, but that it did not mean there was anything wrong with OSU. In a response to a question from Baldwin, Bob answered:

It's not one against the other. People always want to put them against each other. I'm thrilled to back at OU. I get in my car and it's a 10-minute drive. They have a chance to win a na-

tional championship. I knew Larry Coker when he coached at
OSU. I knew Johnny Barr. I knew him when he was a player
at OU, then he was at OSU as a coach, and now we're back at
OU together. [20]

By 1991, Bob had been a sportscaster for more than 30 years
and loved to look back on his career. He had been in the next room
in the OU president's office the day in 1969 when Steve Owens
received a call from the Downtown Athletic Club in New York City
telling him he had won the Heisman Trophy. He also was present with Barry Sanders in Tokyo when it was announced that he
had won the Heisman. Bob said, "I've been very lucky to have the
career I've had." [21]

Bob reflected on the status of college athletics. After OU had
gone through the late 1980s with some players getting into trouble
with the law, critics of college athletics came out of the woodwork.
Bob said:

To say college athletics is bad, and it's bad to win, is wrong.
We're a country that likes to win. What's wrong with that?
Everyone should have to play fair, but there is nothing wrong
with winning. Everywhere I go in the nation, people talk about
Oklahoma, the football team, and our great tradition of win-
ning. So why pick out the bad things about athletics? Concen-
trate on the good kids and the fact that they are winners, both
on the field and after they graduate. [22]

After the 1991 football season, Bob turned his attention to
OU basketball. During the years Bob had been away from OU, the
men's basketball program had gained national prominence under the
watchful eye of head coach Billy Tubbs. A native of Tulsa, Tubbs
coached at his alma mater, Lamar University, before he was hired

Terry Evans is the Sooners' career leader in assists, 3-pointers, and 3-point attempts. He played from 1990 to 1993. *Courtesy University of Oklahoma Athletic Department.*

Billy Tubbs led the Sooners to the national championship game against Kansas in 1988. His 333 wins are the most in OU basketball history. *Courtesy University of Oklahoma Athletic Department.*

as the Sooners' coach. He won the Big Eight Conference championship in 1985, 1988, and 1990. Star players such as Wayman Tisdale, Mookie Blaylock, and Stacey King helped OU to play deeply into the NCAA Tournament under Tubbs, including playing in the 1988 title game in Kansas City. Unfortunately, the Sooners lost the game by four points to the University of Kansas, a team they had beaten twice that season in conference play.

Bob enjoyed broadcasting OU basketball again with the help of color commentator Mark Mathew and producer-engineer Michael Dean. The broadcast team's job was made easier by OU Athletic Director John "Underdog" Underwood who traveled to games with the crew. Underwood, future Associate Commissioner of the Big 12 Conference, said, "It was a wonderful time to work with Bob. He was an incredible professional and obviously loves what he does. There is no doubt Bob has a great passion for Oklahoma."[23]

Coach Tubbs' teams were well-balanced and exciting to watch. The venue also was different. When Bob left as the voice of the Sooners, basketball games were still played in the old fieldhouse. The Lloyd Noble Center was built on the south part of the OU campus in Norman and was named for a former OU regent whose family contributed the first $1 million. The arena opened in 1975 and was sometimes called the "House that Alvin built and Wayman filled," referring to the successes of star forward Alvan Adams and scoring king Wayman Tisdale.[24]

Bob has broadcast both high school and college games from Owen Field on the campus of OU in Norman since 1957. *Courtesy University of Oklahoma Athletic Department.*

CHAPTER TWELVE

Unsettled Times in Norman

It was hard to sound upbeat on the radio when Sooner drives were consistently stopped by turnovers, mistakes, and penalties.

—BOB BARRY

OU Coach Gary Gibbs won 24 of his first 34 games as head coach from 1989 to 1991, but Sooner fans were unhappy. Gibbs was not regularly beating OU's main rivals, Texas, Nebraska, and Colorado.

Bob liked the genial Gibbs who had produced outstanding defenses for a decade for OU. When fans called for Gibbs' firing in 1992, they included Bob with other supporters of the coach. One OU fan wrote *The Daily Oklahoman*, "If Oklahoma President Van Horn, Donnie Duncan, Barry Switzer, and Bob Barry want to keep Gary Gibbs, that's fine. Let them pay $30 a ticket for all the empty seats this season." [1]

Sports talk show listeners debated whether Gibbs should remain. The topic also was hot with letters to newspaper sports editors, especially after Gibbs' Sooners lost to Texas for the fourth consecutive year in October, 1992. An OU fan from Missouri wrote, "After suffering through one more year of OU-Texas football and getting salt poured into our wounds one more time, we must evaluate ourselves, our leadership, and the future of Oklahoma football." [2]

Fans accused Gibbs of being too conservative offensively—others blamed the players, not the coach. An Oklahoma City OU fan wrote, "This year's loss to the Texas Longhorns lies entire on the shoulders of the OU football team, not on coach Gibbs....Remember, you can lead a horse to water, but you can't make him drink. Gary Gibbs is not at fault this year. The Sooner team is." [3]

There was little to cheer about in Norman. Even Bob believed the quality of his and color commentator Mike Treps' broadcasts suffered. Bob said, "When the team was doing so badly, even our broadcasts were negative. It is hard to sound upbeat in game after game with turnovers and penalties stopping Sooner drives." Bob was critical of himself after almost every OU game in the early 1990s. He told himself that if OU was winning big, even his critics would be quieted. He said, "Broadcasts always sound better if your team is winning." [4]

OU fans remember only a few good times in 1992 as the Sooners finished 5-4-2, winning only 5 of 11 games. One of the ties was a 15-15 game against OSU. Aubrey Beavers, a tough linebacker with a great sense of humor that got players through the tough season, said after the OSU tie, "This feels so bad. Finishing tied with OSU isn't like kissing your sister. It's like kissing your ugly twin sisters." [5]

Another humorous moment came in the 1992 spring game which still pitted alumni versus current players. When former Heisman Trophy winner Steve Owens ran 40 yards for a touchdown, Bob told his radio audience that it was the only time an official ever thought of calling a delay of game penalty during a play. Color man Mike Treps said he timed the run and it was more than 40 seconds. [6]

BELOW: Bob, right, not only broadcast OU basketball games during the last few seasons the Sooners were coached by Billy Tubbs, left, they enjoyed each other's company on the golf course.

ABOVE: Bob and close friend, Don Symcox, left, after a round of golf at St. Andrews in Scotland in June, 1993.

The 1993 season was somewhat more successful for Gibbs. After a 5-0 start, and a much-needed 38-17 victory over Texas, the Sooners were ranked in the Top Ten of the Associated Press poll for the first time since 1987. But three conference losses knocked OU out of the national picture. A loss to Nebraska was the final regular season game but OU was invited to the John Hancock Bowl in El Paso, Texas, to play Texas Tech. Cale Gundy was brilliant at quarterback as the Sooners beat the Red Raiders 41-10, capping a 9-3 season. Gundy threw for three touchdowns and finished as OU's all-time leader in just about every statistical passing category. Bob truly thought, "With a 9-3 record and an impressive bowl victory, surely Gibbs has earned the right to coach OU for several more years." Bob was somewhat optimistic about Gibbs' future.[7]

The Sooner Network had some financial problems in 1993. The American Network Group that had won the bid to broadcast OU football and basketball games by promising to pay $2.85 million over a three-year period defaulted. By July, 1993, OU was owed more than $1 million and OU general counsel Fred Gipson vowed to recover the money for the university. Because American Network Group could not hold up its end of the bargain of producing and broadcasting OU games, OU decided to produce its own broadcasts.

RIGHT: Bob Barry, Jr., left, says hello to his father just before the elder Barry begins another OU football broadcast high above Owen Field.

LEFT: In the broadcast booth preparing for an OU game are, left to right, sideline annoucner Mark Mathew, Bob, and color analyst Merv Johnson.

Using the same equipment and satellite to transmit the games to affiliate stations, Bob and his broadcast crew never missed a beat as the new football season unfolded.[8]

The success of Gibbs' Sooners in 1993 did not repeat itself in 1994. OU historian Jay C. Upchurch described Gibbs' problem, "There are so many challenges and expectations when following a legend in the coaching business. Gary Gibbs found that out the hard way." Just when fans who had called for Gibbs' firing because of always losing to Texas were silenced by the OU win in 1993, Texas beat the Sooners 17-10 in 1994. OU lost to Brigham Young University in the Copper Bowl, finishing a disappointing season at 6-6. Gibbs had little support among OU regents and major donors and was fired at the end of the 1994 season. He later was a defensive coach at Georgia, LSU, and for the Dallas Cowboys, New Orleans Saints, and Kansas City Chiefs of the NFL.[9]

OU had a change in its men's basketball program in 1994 when Billy Tubbs decided to resign. OU chose Kelvin Sampson, a North Carolina native who had coached at Montana Tech University and Washington State University. Bob met Sampson at the news conference in Norman and told the new coach he was sports director at Channel Four and, as the radio voice of the basketball team, would be traveling to distant destinations with the team. Sampson said, "At the time I had no idea how close we would become as friends and the incredible respect we would develop for each other." [10]

During the 1994 football season, Bob invited Sampson to the broadcast booth several times to talk about the upcoming basketball team and season. Sampson remembered:

Bob was always trying to promote the basketball team, not just being my new good friend. I knew right away how impor-

*tant football was, but I also knew how sincere Bob was in inter-
viewing me to get fans excited about the basketball season. He
was genuinely excited even if I saw him around town. He was
always talking about the team. As far as I was concerned, Bob's
integrity and professionalism on the job were unquestioned.*[11]

In Sampson's first season, 1994-1995, great things happened
for OU basketball. Listeners could hear the excitement in Bob's
voice as he and Mark Mathew described the action of 15 wins
with no losses at Lloyd Noble Center and a 23-9 overall record.
For the effort, Sampson was named National Coach of the Year by
the Associated Press, the National Basketball Writers Association,
and *Basketball Weekly*. However, the Sooners were knocked out
by 13th-seeded Manhattan College in the first round of the NCAA
Tournament in Memphis, Tennessee. Manhattan was coached by
later ESPN basketball announcer Fran Fraschilla.

Bob, left, and OU foot-
ball coach Howard
Schnellenberger at a
Sooner football banquet.
Schnellenberger's tenure
at OU was short lived.
*Courtesy University of Okla-
homa Athletic Department.*

OU was winning in basketball, but not in football. Listening to fans who did not believe the previous football coach Gibbs was "head-coach" material, OU went after a seasoned coach and hired 61-year-old Howard Schnellenberger who had won a national championship at the University of Miami and had turned around a faltering program at the University of Louisville.

"It was never the right fit," Bob said. On paper, Schnellenberger had vast experience in college football and obviously knew how to turn losing programs into winners. But Schnellenberger misjudged how important the past was to Sooner faithful. Bob said, "He didn't ride the team bus with the players, he always had a car. He also was quoted as saying that he would create a winning team so good that OU fans would forget Bud Wilkinson and Barry Switzer." [12]

Schnellenberger may have been doomed from the beginning because of his lack of interest in the history of OU football. He ordered staff members to throw away old files and destroy flags from previous teams. However, behind his back, wiser assistants archived the material.

Schnellenberger's overconfidence "came back to bite him," said Bob. After the Sooners posted a 5-5-1 record in 1995 and did not get invited to a bowl game, much negative attention was directed at Schnellenberger who was fired by OU President David Boren. In a period of one year, OU again was looking for a new football coach.

From a "seasoned" coach in Schnellenberger, OU went in a completely different direction and hired former OU player John Blake as head coach. Blake had limited coaching experience as an assistant coach at OU for four years and with the Dallas Cowboys for four years. However, he had strong backing for the job from former coach Barry Switzer, OU athletic director Steve Owens, and former OU President George L. Cross.

OU's football fortunes continued to be in the doldrums in 1996 under the new coach, Blake. OU was now competing in the Big 12 Conference, an amalgamation of former teams of the Big Eight Conference and four major universities in Texas. Joining the former Big Eight schools were OU's arch-rival, Texas, Texas A & M University, Baylor University, and Texas Tech University.

Even during less-than-perfect football campaigns, Bob tried to paint a positive picture on radio broadcasts. Bryan Stolte, the spotter for radio broadcasts, said, "Bob would try to look for the positive in every situation. If OU played bad, Bob would talk about some individual player having a good game." As spotter, Stolte constantly pointed to Bob's spotter boards to indicate which players had been involved in the previous play.[13]

At the beginning of Bob's second stint as play-by-play announcer of Sooner football games, he experimented with using two spotters—one for OU and the other for the opponent. Dale Kimsey, an Oklahoma City attorney, had spotted for Bob for several years at OSU and followed him to Norman for a few seasons. Bob's son, Frank, and Lee Thompson, Jr., also had helped out as spotters.[14]

The only bright spot of a 3-8 season for OU in 1996 was a victory over Texas in the Red River Rivalry at the Cotton Bowl in Dallas. Football heroes were hard to find during the low years of the mid-1990s, but James Allen scored from the two-yard line in overtime to clinch a 30-27 win over the Longhorns. Coach Blake's team had entered the Texas game 0-4 and was a 22-point underdog to Texas that was ranked number 25 in the Associated Press poll.[15] Even with the victory over Texas, the 1996 OU football season was the worst, percentage-wise, since 1895.

Bob has been honored at many black-tie events for his half
century of broadcasting OU and OSU football and basketball
games.

In the summer of 1996, Bob made
a career decision. He was 65 years old
and decided to resign as sports director
at Channel Four. His intention was to
remain as a sports reporter, and recommended that his son, Bob Barry, Jr.,
replace him as sports director. That eventually happened, but not for
a year.[16]

Bob's main reason for giving up his full-time job was to spend
more time at home with Joan. "I'm not retiring," Bob told Mel
Bracht of *The Daily Oklahoman*. "I'm going to cut back my assign-
ments so I can be home in the evenings." Bob Barry, Jr., took over
the responsibility for the evening sportscasts.[17]

Bob left the sports director's job with Channel Four in first
place in ratings for every sportscast of the day and in overall pro-
gramming.[18] In announcing his job change, Bob made certain everyone understood that the semi-retirement from Channel Four did
not affect his status as play-by-play announcer for Sooner football
and basketball. When Bob Barry, Jr., was appointed sports director,
he said, "It's kind of fun to be Dad's boss, and tell him what to do
once in awhile." [19]

The next two seasons, 1997 and 1998, saw more losing than
winning on the football field. In 1997, the Sooners were 4-8 and in
1998, OU posted a 5-6 record. It was the first time in Sooner history
that OU had three consecutive losing seasons. Even though Blake
was considered a masterful recruiter of young men who would star

Two veteran broadcasters and a veteran basketball coach at an OU basketball banquet. Left to right, ESPN's Dick Vitale, Bob, and OU men's basketball coach Kelvin Sampson.

on future teams, OU fired him. Later, Blake served as a defensive line coach at Mississippi State University, the University of Nebraska, and the University of North Carolina.

OU fans "were fit to be tied," Bob said. "Since the winning ways of Barry Switzer, no coach for a decade had performed to the expectations of Sooner fans who were showing up in lesser numbers at home games." The negative attitude of many fans toward the team's performance no doubt affected how they perceived the radio broadcast.[20]

Everywhere Bob went, from the coffee shop to the barber shop, OU faithful wanted OU President David Boren to take the lead and hire a winning coach to bring OU football back to its pinnacle as the winningest program since World War II. Jay C. Upchurch wrote, "Oklahoma fans were starving for positives. The Sooners had not posted a winning record in five years, and it seemed more like 500 years."[21]

Bob was inducted into the Oklahoma Journalism Hall of Fame at the University of Central Oklahoma (UCO) in 1998. He was a member of an induction class of giants in journalism in Oklahoma. Joining him in the ceremony were his fellow co-anchor at Channel Four, Linda Cavanaugh; UCO communications department head and curator of the Will Rogers Memorial Reba Collins; well-known western author Fred Grove; legislative reporter Marie Price; newspaper publisher Joe Ferguson; and pioneer newsreel photographer Arthur Ramsey. William Ross was honored posthumously as the editor of the state's first newspaper, the *Cherokee Advocate*, in Indian Territory in 1844.[22]

LEFT: University of Oklahoma President David Boren, left, has been a strong supporter of Bob continuing as the voice of the Sooners.

BELOW: Bob, standing, at one of many banquets he attended each year as voice of the two major sports at OU. Left to right, men's basketball coach Kelvin Sampson, his wife, Karen Sampson, and OU Athletic Director Joe Castiglione.

Also in 1998, former OU and Green Bay Packers tight end Keith Jackson joined the OU football broadcast team. For the first and only time in OU broadcast history, there were three announcers in the booth. Bob still did play-by-play and Mike Treps and Jackson provided color commentary. Bob told reporters he was excited about the challenge of having three men in the booth. Bob knew that Jackson was a likeable former player who had close ties to the OU coaching staff.[23]

In 1998, Bob appeared at a charity golf tournament at Oak Tree Country Club with former New York Yankee pitcher Roger Clemens, left.

It was the last year of a contract for broadcast rights held by Diamond-Learfield, a joint venture of Diamond Broadcasting and Learfield Sports. Jackson's hiring fueled speculation that a new successful bidder for the rights might want to replace Bob as the voice of the Sooners. OU announced it was opening bids for a new contract for broadcast rights, although the new successful bidder would be handling more than just radio broadcasts of football and basketball games. The new approach would include radio, game-day sponsorships, the Internet, and coaches shows.

Leading the public campaign to get rid of Bob was media columnist Mel Bracht of *The Daily Oklahoman*.[24] In a column titled, "It's Time for Barry to Sign Off as OU Radio Voice," Bracht openly criticized Bob's call of football games. Calling Bob a legend, Bracht said, "Let's hope the new contract winning bidder will agree to make a change in the play-by-play announcer…It's time for a change." Bracht got right to the point, suggesting that former OU broadcaster John Brooks or David Garrett be named voice of the Sooners.[25]

Another item of change on the horizon for the OU football broadcast team was Mike Treps' retirement as color commentator. In November, 1998, Treps provided color for the Texas Tech game, finishing 24 years on Sooner broadcasts. Before the game, Bob told sports reporter Berry Tramel, "I just can't say enough nice things about Mike. If you endure long enough, people feel like they've come to know you. The longer you're associated with a school, especially if they are winning, they love you." [26]

Unfortunately, OU football teams were not winning and those who supported and ran the juggernaut known as Sooner football were poised for a change.

CHAPTER THIRTEEN

On Top Again

*It's always easier to broadcast sporting events when your team
has magic and has a chance of winning every contest.
The revival of OU football and basketball gave me new life as
the voice of the Sooners.*

—BOB BARRY

A new winning era in OU football actually began before a
new head coach was hired. Earlier in 1998, OU President Boren
personally convinced University of Missouri Athletic Director Joe
Castiglione to bring his talents to Norman. A University of Maryland graduate, Castiglione had spent 17 years in the athletic department at Missouri, the last five as the director. He was credited with
rebuilding Missouri sports and excelled in hiring good coaches,
raising money for the program, and creating an innovative plan for
facilities.

Castiglione took over as OU athletic director just a few months
before John Blake was fired as head football coach. In the past,
large committees were formed to help select a new coach. This time
was different. President Boren said, "We have hired a professional
athletic director and I trust him to consider a small, but highly-qual-
ified pool of candidates."[1]

Through an intense process, and in close consultation with Boren, Castiglione narrowed the field to two candidates. One of the candidates was the defensive coordinator at the University of Florida, Robert Anthony "Bob" Stoops. Very few OU fans had heard of Stoops. Jay C. Upchurch said, "Outside of coaching circles, Stoops was not exactly a household name. Sure, he had developed into one of the top defensive coordinators in the country, but that did not guarantee him much in the way of publicity, at least outside Florida." [2]

Bob learned that Stoops was one of ten children whose father coached all of his sons at Cardinal Mooney High School in Youngstown, Ohio. Stoops was an All-Big Ten Conference defensive back at the University of Iowa and was an assistant coach for

Joe Castiglione became athletic director at OU in 1998 after rebuilding sports programs at the University of Missouri. *Courtesy University of Oklahoma Athletic Department.*

the Hawkeyes, Kent State University, and Kansas State University
before being hired as defensive coordinator by head coach Steve
Spurrier at Florida in 1996.[3]

Rumors were that Stoops was the choice of Boren and that he
had accepted the job after he met at the Dallas-Fort Worth Airport
with Boren, Castiglione, and prominent former players and supporters. On December 1, 1998, Stoops was introduced as the new
head football coach. Bob said, "Somehow, everyone associated with
the program believed in this 38-year-old new coach who brought a
sense of real professionalism and hard-work ethic to Norman."[4]

While Stoops was putting together a top-flight staff and recruiting new players to join the Blake-recruited stars such as Josh
Norman, Roy Williams, Rocky Calmus, and J.T. Thatcher, Bob
was receiving more awards for his long and distinguished career in
broadcasting. At the winter convention of the Oklahoma Association of Broadcasters (OAB) in Tulsa in February, Bob was inducted
into the OAB Hall of Fame, joining such notables as Paul Harvey
and Gene Autry.[5]

When he learned he was chosen for the Hall of Fame, Bob said,
"To even be mentioned in the same breath with the likes of Paul
Harvey and Gene Autry on the national scene is completely mind-
boggling." Bob said it was the greatest honor he ever had received.
At the awards ceremony, Bob told the audience that he had never
been employed fulltime in any industry except broadcasting. He
said, "Broadcasting has been good to my family and me. It has offered me a great, fun life."[6]

In addition to having a new head coach, the radio broadcasts
of Sooner sports experienced a lot of change. The football and basketball broadcasts on radio were part of Sooner Sports Properties,

a joint venture of Learfield Communications, Renda Broadcasting, and Griffin Television.

Also, Bob had a new sidekick in the broadcast booth for the 1999 season. Former OU assistant head football coach Merv Johnson joined the broadcast team that included Bob and sideline reporter Mark Mathew. Johnson replaced the retiring Treps and Keith Jackson who was seeking a television analyst job such as he had in a former stint as an analyst for Turner Network Television games. Jackson ended up on the radio broadcast team at the University of Arkansas.

Bob casually had known Johnson for many years because their wives worked together at The Snappy Fox, a Norman women's clothing store. Bob liked Johnson's honesty, down-to-earth analysis, and good nature. Johnson, a football and academic star at the University of Missouri, had been associated with OU football since 1979 when he joined Coach Switzer's staff as offensive line coach. In 1998, he was named director of football operations and coordinated off-the-field activities of Sooner players and dealt with on-campus recruiting visits. "With the daily contact with players," Bob said, "Merv was familiar with each player's position and responsibilities during the game. I knew from the beginning he and I would click as a broadcast team." [7]

Before their first broadcast, Bob and Johnson met several times to talk about working together. Johnson already had seen firsthand Coach Stoops returning a sense of urgency and an attitude that would promote positive results. Johnson said, "We may not win a championship every year, but we should always be a factor in the conference race." Johnson had been recruiting coordinator in the 1997 and 1998 seasons and stayed close to the team but became more involved in the administrative aspects of coaching. Jay C. Upchurch said OU was fortunate that Johnson stayed in the program after Coach Switzer left, "The ten seasons between Switzer's departure in 1988 and Stoops' arrival in 1999 were the most taxing of Johnson's 40-plus-year career as a coach. Not only was he passed over as Switzer's successor, he had to endure one of the darkest periods in OU football annals." [8]

Bob and Merv Johnson, left, made up a cogent broadcast team. Bob sports a sombrero on one of the Sooner trips to San Diego to play in the Holiday Bowl.

In the summer before the new football season, Bob had to go through another round of Mel Bracht at *The Oklahoman* predicting that 1999 would be Bob's last. On June 3, Bracht wrote, "a source close to the athletic department said this season likely will be his farewell tour." Bracht reported that athletic director Castiglione appeared to be leaning toward replacing Bob, but "Barry's friends and coaches at the university, including basketball coach Kelvin Sampson, lobbied that he get another season." [9] Bracht was wrong about one thing. He failed to mention that OU President Boren, a man who is known for undying loyalty, supported Bob 100 percent. Even if some people wanted Bob replaced, Boren was not about to do it.

Andrew Gilman wrote an intriguing article in *The Oklahoman* three weeks later. Titled "On the Defensive," Gilman gave Bob a chance to answer critics. He wrote:

Bob Barry, Sr., is facing fourth-and-long...Half the crowd loves it and half the crowd hates it...His heels are on his own goal line. The goalposts shade him. But he's not punting. No way. This fall, there will be football. And Barry will be there, in the broadcast booth, fighting for his livelihood.

Talk radio rips him; newspapers, too. Everyone claims to know what the 68-year-old Barry should do. He's slowed down. Lost a step. Once he was great, now his time has passed. Others disagree, arguing that he is a link to the past. Part of Oklahoma history, a link to Steve Owens and Lucious Selmon, Crimson and Cream.[10]

Bob defended himself. "You have to have thick skin," he said. "You must be honest with yourself enough to known when you are slipping...You are going to make mistakes when you are talking for three hours." Castiglione also defended Bob. As an athletic department administrator for nearly two decades, Castiglione said he had fielded criticism of announcers for a long time, but admitted he had never heard some of the types of personal criticism of Bob. Castiglione said, "Much of it is unfounded, because Bob is a super individual and a consummate professional." [11]

Bob, always showing kindness to his detractors, said:

The criticism is not all unfair. But no one likes it. I read the newspaper. I listen to the radio. I know guys like Jim Traber [a host of WWLS, the Sports Animal] hate my guts. I know it's not personal, they just don't like the way I call games...The Sooners' funk has something to do with the attacks on me.

Bob is congratulated on his induction into the Oklahoma Sports Hall of Fame by Oklahoma Governor Frank Keating, left, and First Lady Cathy Keating.

Believe me, if OU had been 8-2 last season, I would have had much less criticism." [12]

Bob also believed that much of the criticism leveled at his play-by-play came from OU fans that never had forgiven him for broadcasting OSU games for 18 years.

Bob's son, BBJ, was quick to defend his father who he called "the legend" on his morning sports talk show on WWLS. BBJ said, "It makes me mad when people severely criticize him. He's my Dad and he still has what it takes to provide a great description of OU football and basketball games to fans listening on the radio." [13]

Callers to "Sports Sound Off" in *The Oklahoman* were evenly split on Bob staying in the broadcast booth. One caller said, "Bob was great, but he's slipping." Still another reader said, "I think Bob should stay. I love it when he says 'Touchdown Oklahoma!' It would be a serious mistake to get rid of him." Another reader, apparently disgusted with all the talk about whether Bob should stay or retire, said, "Is anyone else tired of this discussion? They could let Elmer Fudd do the games if OU started winning. That's what the fans really care about!" [14]

In the middle of the public debate over Bob's future, he
received his greatest honor and the highest award available for anyone connected with sports in Oklahoma. In August, 1999, Bob was
inducted into the Oklahoma Sports Hall of Fame, along with golfer
Orville Moody, football star Jerry Tubbs, and veteran basketball
coach Don Haskins, at a star-studded banquet at the Marriott Hotel
in Oklahoma City. He joined 58 other Oklahomans who excelled
in the world of sports, including Jim Thorpe, Mickey Mantle, Carl
Hubbell, Henry Iba, Warren Spahn, Abe Lemons, and the Waner
brothers, Lloyd and Paul. The Sports Hall of Fame was founded in
1986, the idea of sportscaster Mick Cornett, who joined forces with
Lynne Draper at the Jim Thorpe Association to give Oklahoma one
of the best sports halls of fame in the nation.[15]

With the summer spent talking about Bob's presence in the
booth, OU fans could not wait for the season to begin. Stoops
hired his brother, Mike, as defensive coordinator and chose Mike
Leach as offensive coordinator. Leach was an offensive genius who
turned the Big 12 upside down with his wide-open offense. Leach
built his offense around the pass and Josh Heupel, a junior college
quarterback recruited to Norman by the new coaching staff, was the
beneficiary. Heupel rewrote most OU passing records during the
1999 season. The fans loved it, so did the players. Trent Smith said,
"Coach Leach has no inhibitions when it comes to calling plays. He
is not afraid to do anything at any time in a game, no matter what
the situation is." [16]

Coach Stoops led his 1999 Sooners to a seven-win season
and took OU to a bowl game for the first time in four years. OU
swamped three non-conference opponents and lost by four points to
Notre Dame at South Bend. Bob said, "It was a breath of fresh air

for a program that had fallen from being a perennial powerhouse to being the league doormat." [17]

Bob and Coach Stoops developed an excellent working relationship early in Stoops' tenure at the university. Stoops said, "I loved Bob's great knowledge of both Sooner history and the entire history of sports in Oklahoma." Stoops immediately recognized Bob's integrity. He remembered, "It takes a rare individual who can manage to work for a local media company as their sports anchor and then serve as the voice of the athletic programs at the state's two largest universities." [18]

OU played in the Independence Bowl on December 31, 1999, against the University of Mississippi. It was the last American sporting event of the millennium and Bob was excited about being at the microphone for such an historic event. Berry Tramel wrote in *The Oklahoman*:

> *It's fitting that Oklahoma-Mississippi is the 1900's last game. What could be more American than an OU-Ole Miss matchup?... Their stories are very much the stories of 20th century America. The 20th century is an Oklahoma century, more than any other American state. The great imprint on Oklahoma psyches, the Dust Bowl and the Depression, was challenged by another Oklahoma phenomenon, Sooner football. Oklahoma football is a frontier success story.* [19]

The post-game show wrapped up about 20 minutes before midnight and the new millennium. Bob and the others sat around the press box until midnight, hoping that predictions that all computers in the world would crash and America would go dark were unfounded. Fortunately, at the stroke of midnight, the lights in the stadium stayed on and Bob and his crew left for their hotel.

LEFT: Eduardo Najera averaged more than 18 points per game in OU's wins over Arizona and UNC Charlotte in the 1999 NCAA Tournament. *Courtesy University of Oklahoma Athletic Department.*

BELOW: In 2000, OU Associate Athletic Department Media Relations Director Mike Houck, right, became color commentator for OU basketball games on the Sooner Radio Network. He and Bob followed the Sooners wherever their wins took them. *Courtesy University of Oklahoma Athletic Department.*

OU basketball also was doing well. OU did well in 1999-2000 on the hardwood. After a good regular season, OU, as a 13th-seed, beat fourth-seeded Arizona and fifth-seeded North Carolina-Charlotte before losing to top-seeded Michigan State in the Sweet Sixteen of the NCAA Tournament. Bob traveled with the team to Milwaukee, Wisconsin, and St. Louis, Missouri, to provide play-by-play of Sooner basketball on the Sooner Network.

Bob and men's basketball coach Kelvin Sampson had grown to be very close friends. "Bob's greatest quality," Sampson said, "is his passion and love for the university. The thing I most loved about Bob was the way he loved his family. He and I both share the view that regardless of what we've accomplished or failed in, the thing we hold most dear to us will always be our family." [20]

A Magical Year

Bob is the best home team announcer that has ever lived.
Even if we played a bad game, he found some positive to talk about.
—KELVIN SAMPSON

OU started the new millennium with a bang. Not only did the
OU basketball team make it to the Sweet Sixteen of the NCAA
Tournament, but pundits on sports radio and sportswriters predicted
the 2000 season might be very special for the football Sooners.
They were right.

Second-year coach Stoops, yet to see his 40th birthday, lost his
offensive coordinator Mike Leach, who left to become head coach
at Texas Tech, but the OU offense rolled on behind new offensive
coordinator Mark Mangino and quarterback Josh Heupel who
would finish second in the Heisman Trophy balloting at the end of
the season. OU began the season ranked number 20 in the Associated Press poll.

The high excitement level as a play-by-play announcer could
be heard in Bob's voice as OU was undefeated at 4-0 going into
a pivotal game against Texas at the Cotton Bowl. As if the annual
battle against the Longhorns was not enough, Sooner fans looked at
the schedule. After the game against number 11 Texas, OU played

number 2 Kansas State and top-ranked Nebraska. Even the most
faithful OU fan dared to think that the Sooners could win all three
games against such a high level of competition. Winning one of the
three games would be great, two masterful, and three—no one really gave OU a chance at the hat trick. [1]

Bob traveled to Dallas for the OU-Texas game in what became
known as "Red October." Before the game, he visited with coaches
and players and hundreds of fans milling around the Cotton Bowl.
"I felt a special sense of excitement among players and fans that
day. I would have been surprised had OU lost to Texas that afternoon." The feeling was correct as OU thrashed Texas 63-14. A week
later, OU beat Kansas State in Manhattan, ending the Wildcats'
home winning streak at 25, and closed out the month by coming
back from a 14-0 deficit to upset number one Nebraska 31-14. Bob
said, "It was one of the greatest months in OU football history and
I was honored to be at the microphone telling fans what was going
on." [2] OU moved from number 10 to number one in the Associated
Press poll in October.

Bob was not the only broadcaster who was impressed with
OU's performance in the month of October. ESPN's Kirk Herbstreit
said, "That was as impressive of run as you'll ever see. OU left little
doubt about who the number one team in the country was at that
point." [3]

After a 56-7 road win over Baylor, OU traveled to College
Station, Texas, to play Texas A & M at Kyle Field, the home of the
"12th man" and one of the toughest venues for a visiting team. Bob
arrived at College Station a day early and walked around the stadium that was storied in college football. He was expecting a good
game between OU and Texas A & M, but had no idea how OU's

perfect season would be in danger most of the day.[4]

The Sooners trailed 24-10 early in the fourth quarter and Sooner coaches hoped for something that would bail out the struggling OU offense and create a spark to change the momentum. That spark came when linebacker Torrance Marshall intercepted an A & M pass and returned it 41 yards for a touchdown. Bob called the action as OU outscored the Aggies 22-7 in the final quarter and made superb defensive stands to preserve a 35-31 victory. On the postgame show, quarterback Josh Heupel said, "Sometimes during the course of a season, many football teams find themselves in a game where they are not playing their best football, and you've got to find a way to win. This football team found a way to win today."

With OU at the top of both polls, the Sooners were targets for opponents in the two remaining regular season games and the Big 12 championship game. OU beat Texas Tech by only 14 points in Norman and won the Bedlam Game at Stillwater against OSU by the close score of 12-7. Then, on December 2, the Sooners beat Kansas State in a rematch of their regular season game 27-24, largely on the arm and with the leadership of quarterback Heupel. Coach Stoops said on the post-game show, "Josh is the complete package. He can do things physically in a great way and there aren't many quarterbacks out there with his instincts and overall intelligence."[5]

Completing the regular season atop the Bowl Championship Series (BCS) ranking, OU earned the right to play Florida State University for the BCS national championship on January 3, 2001, at the Orange Bowl in Miami, Florida. OU's Heupel was pitted against Florida State signal-caller Chris Weinke who had beaten Heupel in the Heisman Trophy balloting. Before the game, Bob interviewed Coach Stoops, who was exceptionally confident of his

Sooners' chances. Bob said, "He had been defensive coordinator at Florida and knew tendencies of Florida State." Stoops looked at Bob during the interview and said, "You're uptight Bob! Don't worry! We gonna be okay!"

The OU radio broadcast crew minutes after the Sooners won the national championship in January, 2001. Left to right, spotter Bryan Stolte, Bob, producer-engineer Michael Dean, color analyst Merv Johnson, and statistician Terry McLemore.

Before the game, OU players were overheard promising to "take back the Heisman" by winning the game and the national championship for Heupel. Sooner Magic was at an all-time high as the Sooners beat Florida State 13-2 and won a seventh national championship in a perfect 13-0 season.

The Daily Oklahoman editorialized:

With seven national championships, every generation of fans likes to think the team in front of them is special and better than those in any of the glorious seasons that came before. But the Sooners of 2000 likely will be a special star in the constellation, because they returned the program to football's mountaintop after dismal years in the valley.[6]

Josh Heupel finished second in the Heisman Trophy balloting in 2000 before leading the Sooners to a national championship with a victory over Florida State University. *Courtesy University of Oklahoma Athletic Department.*

OU coach Bob Stoops hoists the national championship trophy after the January, 2001 victory over Florida State University. Stoops said the best thing about working with Bob Barry is his "fantastic sense of humor." Stoops said, "He's one of the rare people I've met who never seems to have a bad day. His quick wit and ability to tell a joke are always welcome to me, especially during a busy football season."

Despite rumors to the contrary, Bob was again named play-by-play announcer for the Sooners in January, 2001. Athletic Director Castiglione said it was important that OU have continuity after one of the biggest football seasons in OU history. Castiglione said in a news release, "We look forward to working with Bob for another season. We appreciate his loyalty to OU athletics and our broadcast properties." OU President Boren also was extremely supportive of Bob in making the announcement. Boren said:

Bob Barry in many ways represents the best of our Sooner spirit. He is no fair weather fan. In good times and bad times, he has been a loyal and enthusiastic Sooner supporter. It's only right that he should do the play-by-play in this year when OU reigns as National Champion.[7]

Bob appreciated the public support of OU officials. He said, "I have really been energized by the success of the football team. I look forward to working another season with Merv Johnson, who I consider one of the most knowledgeable analysts I have ever shared a radio booth with." [8]

Bob knew that the 2000 season would be difficult to duplicate, especially because quarterback Heupel was gone. In conversations with his friends, however, he found OU fans to expect another national championship. Coach Stoops' success had bred incredible expectations. In the first game of the season, Bob found himself believing that OU football had returned to the pinnacle of college sports in a magical way, especially when defensive tackle recruit Tommie Harris dropped a North Carolina running back for a three-yard loss on the first play of the 2001 season.[9]

The Sooners averaged 40 points per game in beating North Carolina, Air Force, and North Texas University without very much resistance. However, OU won by a single point over Kansas State, setting up another Cotton Bowl battle against Texas. It was a game Bob would never forget, especially when he made the call late in the game when Sooner defensive back Roy Williams launched himself over a blocker and batted down a Texas quarterback Chris Simms' pass into the waiting arms of linebacker Teddy Lehman who took three steps and scored a touchdown.[10]

There was another reason Bob remembers the call in the OU victory over the Longhorns. It was the day future Heisman Trophy winner Jason White replaced quarterback Nate Hybl after he was hurt. White played well in backup duty, giving Sooner fans something to cheer about for the future.[11]

OU continued its perfect season with wins over Kansas and Baylor before suffering its first loss, 20-10, to Nebraska on a late trick play that really began Cornhusker quarterback Eric Crouch's run for the Heisman Trophy. Bob was the first to tell Sooner fans listening on radios around the state that Jason White was injured, and a cold Nate Hybl came back into the game.

OU won three consecutive games as blowouts over Tulsa, Texas A & M, and Texas Tech before losing to Bedlam rival OSU

Bob and the Sooner Football Network team broadcast the OU-Arkansas Cotton Bowl game on January 1, 2002. The OU crew welcomed to the booth former OU All-American tight end and, after his retirement from professional football, Sooner Network color analyst Keith Jackson. In the 2001 season, Jackson joined the broadcast crew for University of Arkansas football broadcasts. In front, Jake Fisher. Second row, left to right, Merv Johnson, Keith Jackson, and Bob. Back row, Jeff Couch, Michael Dean, Terry McLemore, and Ron Benton.

16-13 on a day when the OU offense fizzled. With a 9-3 record, OU was invited to play in the Cotton Bowl on New Year's Day against the University of Arkansas.

While celebrating OU's 10-3 victory over Arkansas in a defensive battle on a bitterly-cold day in the Cotton Bowl, Bob had another major sports story to deal with in Norman. University of Florida coach Steve Spurrier resigned to become head coach of the Washington Redskins of the NFL. National media immediately began speculating that OU Coach Stoops was number one on the list to replace Spurrier. To Bob, there was a good chance that Stoops might return to the program where he was defensive coordinator. He had won a national championship and was taking OU to three consecutive bowl games, and was "hot property" for schools such as Florida that were looking for a new head coach.[12]

Bob learned that Florida indeed had contacted Stoops and that he was giving "great consideration" to the possibility of returning as head coach of the Gators. Bob already had gained great respect for Stoops as a good family man and knew the coach would consider what was best for his wife and children. Television crews and reporters shadowed Stoops' office as the coach and his wife agonized over the decision.

At a news conference, Stoops announced his decision:
From time to time, people have choices in their lives as to what they want to do. I want to clarify and straighten out so many of the wrong rumors that have been out there recently. I feel committed to what we're doing at Oklahoma, about the strength of our program, and where it's heading. I feel that is what's most important to me is to continue to develop this program at Oklahoma.[13]

After the news conference was broadcast live on radio and television, a sigh of relief could be heard from OU fans all over the state. Bob believed part of the reason Stoops stayed because he believed "OU was a place at which you can win and win big." [14]

As soon as Bob put away his spotter board from the football season in early 2002, he resumed broadcasting OU basketball

The Sooner Network radio crew at the Final Four in March, 2002. Left to right, producer-engineer Michael Dean, color analyst Mike Houck, and Bob.

games. Coach Kelvin Sampson had his Sooners flying high on their way to a second seed in the NCAA Tournament. Bob accompanied the Sooners hoops squad to Dallas where OU won against the University of Illinois-Chicago and Xavier University in the first two rounds of the tournament. Then the venue changed to San Diego and a 21-point OU win over Arizona in the Sweet Sixteen. The San Diego air was kind to the Sooners as they beat Missouri 81-75 in the Elite Eight to earn a trip to Final Four in Atlanta, Georgia. Before more than 50,000 fans in Atlanta, OU lost to Indiana 73-64, ending the best OU basketball season since 1988 when the Sooners played Kansas in the national championship game.

Coach Sampson appreciated Bob because of his positive attitude. "He could make a positive out of nothing," Sampson said. "Sometimes I would walk away from a post-game interview trying to figure out if we really lost the game or not. We might have played our worst game in the history of round bouncing ball, but Bob would find something positive like, 'Coach, don't you think this guy had his best game of the year?'" [15]

Sometimes after a less-than-stellar Sooner performance, Bob would say, "Coach, the other team could not have played better—it seemed like they could hit their shots blind-folded!" After such comments, Sampson, would walk away thinking, "Bob, I wish you would let me be mad at my team instead of making me think they weren't that bad that night!" [16]

OU football was a pre-season pick to win the national championship in at least one publication when the 2002 football season began. The Sooners were 4-0 before beating Texas 35-24 and blowing out Iowa State and Colorado. OU, ranked number one, went into College Station again to play Texas A & M. The unranked Aggies beat OU, led by freshman quarterback Reggie McNeal.

Bob saw the Sooners come back with vengeance and beat Baylor and Texas Tech by huge margins. The week before the OSU game, OU had moved back to number three in the Associated Press poll. The Cowboys were ready in an ambush for the Sooners, going up 35-6 before OU began to move the ball. OSU won the game 38-28 and all hopes of returning to a national championship game were over for the Sooners.

OU beat Colorado in the Big 12 Championship 29-7 and earned a berth in the Rose Bowl against Washington State University. Quarterback Nate Hybl starred in the game and Oklahoma won

34-14, finishing the season at number three in the BCS.

The OU men's basketball team excelled again in the season that ended in the spring of 2003. OU won the Big 12 Conference tournament championship for the second year in a row with Hollis Price leading the team in scoring for a second consecutive year. The Sooners went all the way to the Elite Eight in the NCAA Tournament with wins over South Carolina State, California, and Butler before losing to top-seeded Syracuse. Bob enjoyed the venue for the top-seeded Sooners who played their first two games in the friendly confines of the Ford Center in Oklahoma City. After the first two wins, OU moved on the regional championship in Albany, New York. "I had rather call a game in Oklahoma City so I could return home for the night, than in upstate New York," Bob said. [17]

Joan and Bob gasp as Bobby presents them a
huge family portrait of the Barry family at Christmas in 2002.

Joan was the love of Bob's life. His closest friends came to his support when he lost Joan in 2003. She died of a rare disease known as Alpha 1.

Joan right, with her close friend, Louise Symcox of Norman.

The spring of 2003 was a sad time for Bob. He helplessly watched as Joan's health deteriorated. For many years she had suffered from a rare, hereditary disease known as Alpha-1 Antitrypsin Deficiency (Alpha-1), a condition that had taken the life of her father. Alpha-1 is a disorder caused by a deficiency of a protein that protects the lungs from diseases such as emphysema, and is often misdiagnosed as such.[18]

Joan had been on oxygen 24-hours-a-day for two years. On the evening of June 10, she was struggling to breathe and asked for medication. When Bob asked her if she wanted to go to the hospital, Joan said, "Not yet." Those were her last words—she died shortly thereafter.[19]

Not long after Joan's death, Bob was scheduled to interview Coach Kelvin Sampson. "In the past," Sampson said, "Bob always came in, and in a businesslike manner, turned on his tape recorder and started asking questions. However, Joan's death so devastated Bob, he just wanted to talk about her and what a wonderful mother and wife she had been." Sampson and his wife, Karen, and Bob and Joan had become very good friends and Sampson knew how much Bob missed his wife of more than 50 years.[20]

When Bob seemingly was ready to do the interview, he turned on the tape recorder, and "nothing came out." He took a moment to gain his composure, then the interview began. Sampson said, "I could see in his eyes how much he missed Joan. Here this veteran sportscaster stood in front of me not able to say a word because of his terrible loss."[21]

In September, 2003, Bob was among the guests for the taping of "Oklahoma Football Legends Reunion," a legendary production by Larry Black that included unforgettable moments with dozens of Sooner football players spanning generations. The video was taped in Tuscaloosa, Alabama, as OU prepared to play Alabama. Bob, Merv Johnson, and former coach Barry Switzer joined 31 former players including Claude Arnold, Brian Bosworth, Steve Davis, Jack Mildren, Billy Sims, Spencer Tillman, Dewey Selmon, Uwe von Schamann, Joe Washington, and Steve Zabel.[22]

Jason White won the Heisman Trophy as the nation's outstanding college football player in 2003. He was the third Heisman winner for whom Bob called the action as play-by-play announcer for either OU or OSU. *Courtesy University of Oklahoma Athletic Department.*

The 2003 football season was a unique season for Bob. It was the third season in which he called every play of a Heisman Trophy winner. Behind Jason White's impeccable passing, the Sooners were the highest scoring team in OU's history, scoring 601 points to only 214 for opponents. That record later was eclipsed by the 2008 team. "I ran out of adjectives to describe scoring drives," Bob remembered. OU had seven games of scoring more than 50 points, including a 77-0 victory over Texas A & M.

After a 12-0 regular season campaign, OU was heavily favored over Kansas State in the Big 12 championship game. Fans said it was the greatest OU team in history. However, before the game it was announced that OU co-defensive coordinator Mike Stoops, the head coach's brother, had been named football coach at the University of Arizona. In the Big 12 game, OU scored first and Bob believed the Sooners would end up winning big like they had most of the season. However, the Sooners had not been seriously challenged to that point in the season and eventually lost to the Wildcats 35-7.

Even with the defeat, OU was still atop the BCS and was invited to the Sugar Bowl in New Orleans to play in the BCS national championship game. Bob knew that quarterback White was "beat up" from previous games. The Louisiana State University defense was too much for the heralded Sooner offense and the Tigers won 21-14. Bob sensed the great disappointment in OU fans that he saw both in New Orleans and back in Norman.[23]

Bob liked White, a "common, every day young man who was not afraid to work hard to accomplish his goals." White, from nearby Tuttle, Oklahoma, not only won the Heisman Trophy in 2003, he also was named Player of the Year by the Associated Press, CNN, and *The Sporting News* and won the Davey O'Brien Award as the nation's outstanding quarterback. "White was a real winner," Bob said. White was 27-4 as a starting quarterback at OU.[24]

The basketball Sooners had a down year in 2003-2004 with a 20-11 record and an appearance in the NIT. In 2004-2005, OU rebounded with a 25-8 record, was Big 12 co-champion, and made it back to the NCAA Tournament. Bob traveled with the team to Tucson, Arizona, where the third-seed Sooners beat Niagara University in the first round, then lost to the University of Utah.

In 2004, the Sooners again went 12-0 in the regular season, beat Colorado 42-3 in the Big 12 Conference championship, then "laid an egg" in the BCS national championship game against the University of Southern California, losing to the Trojans 55-19. It was one of the most disappointing games Bob ever called as the voice of the Sooners.

Even after 48 years in the broadcast booth, Bob experienced a "first" in October, 2004. Just before the start of the fourth quarter in the game against Kansas at Owen Field, Bob experienced a broadcaster's worst fear—he lost his voice. Bob had come down with a cold on Friday night before the game and "saw it coming." He felt great, but by the fourth quarter, when he opened his mouth, he had no voice.[25]

Bob tried everything—downing bottles of Sprite and sucking eucalyptus cough drops and lemon wedges that were retrieved from the catering crew. Producer-engineer Michael Dean called down to the field from the sixth-floor radio booth and summoned sideline reporter Mark Rodgers to do the play-by-play for the fourth quarter and handle the post-game show. After the broadcast ended, Rodgers, a native Oklahoman who grew up in Blackwell and became a local celebrity on the Sports Animal and KOCO-TV, said, "You've got to get better. It's hard to replace the guy who's been doing this for 100 years." Bob told a reporter, "My voice has got to get better by morning. I'm supposed to read at church tomorrow." [26]

Also in 2004, Bob received the Bill Teegins Excellence in Sportscasting Award, a prestigious honor named for Teegins, the former OSU play-by-play announcer who was killed with nine other OSU basketball players and athletic department staff in a January, 2001 airplane crash en route to Stillwater from Boulder, Colorado. Previous winners of the award included major league baseball announcers Joe Simpson, Bobby Murcer, and Curt Gowdy.

In August, 2005, Bob was featured in an story in *The Oklahoman* under the headline, "No Signs of Stopping." Mel Bracht wrote:

Five years after announcing he planned to retire and then changing his mind, Bob Barry, Sr., shows no signs of wanting to hang up the microphone as the radio voice of the Sooners football and basketball games. [27]

Bob gave much of the credit for his longevity to his broadcast partner, Merv Johnson. Bob said, "Working with Merv has just been a boon to my existence. He knows so much about the game we blend together well." [28]

The newspaper story brought out another round of anti-Bob letter writers whose theme was generally "It's time for Bob to go." However, an OU fan from Beaumont, Texas, wrote:

Remember Walter Cronkite? His was a reassuring voice and he was revered like your favorite uncle. Like Bob Barry. All is well with Bob, and his experiences, making like an old pair of house shoes—comfortable and indispensible. Bob makes mistakes every now and then. Let's see here, don't we all? Part of his charisma is, like Cronkite, giving the listener a feeling that basically all is good hands even if it is fourth-and-12 for the Sooners. [29]

Another reader said, "We tune in the game on television but mute the sound and listen to Barry's always enthusiastic play-by-play. I hope he is on the radio for years to come." Still another fan said, "I have talked to Bob from time to time, and he has been nothing but friendly and gracious...He and Merv are Oklahoma and that's what counts." [30]

The OU football team was 8-4 in 2005, posting the worst season record since 1999. The year started out badly with a loss to Texas Christian University and the Sooners were 2-3 after the first five games, including losses to UCLA and Texas. The Sooners finished 22nd in the Associated Press poll after beating Oregon in the Holiday Bowl in San Diego, California.

Toward the end of the 2005 season, OU lost to Texas Tech on a controversial play. Bob "tries not to be a complete homer," but recognizes that 90 percent of the audience listening to an OU game is made up of Sooner fans. At the end of the Texas Tech game, Bob said, "I didn't say Texas Tech won, the officials said they won." Afterwards, Bob was apologetic, "I just completely lost it, there were so many screw-ups. I was not pleased with the way I reported it, but it got to me. OU lost the game only because of an official's call." [31]

CHAPTER FIFTEEN

Still Going Strong

*When Bob began broadcasting major college football games,
man had not yet gone into space and ESPN for avid sports fans
was still two decades away.*

—LEE ALLAN SMITH

Bob was a larger-than-life hero when I was growing up.
—BILL HANCOCK
Executive Director, Bowl Championship Series (BCS)

Bob lost a good friend at OU when basketball coach Kelvin
Sampson was named head coach at Indiana University in March,
2006. Sampson had guided the Sooners to eight seasons with 20 or
more wins and has the highest winning percentage in OU history
(.721). In his final six seasons in Norman, Sampson averaged 26
wins per year and had the best record in the Big 12 Tournament
among league coaches.

Sampson was replaced by Jeff Capel, III, a starting guard on
the Duke University basketball team for four years. Capel was from
a basketball family. His father, Jeff Capel, II, was head coach at Old
Dominion University and assistant coach for the Charlotte Bobcats
of the NBA. Before coming to OU, the younger Capel was head

coach at Virginia Commonwealth University. At the Virginia school, Capel guided the Rams to a record number of wins.

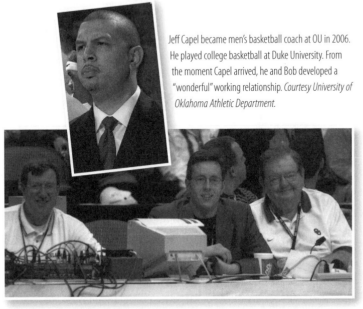

Jeff Capel became men's basketball coach at OU in 2006. He played college basketball at Duke University. From the moment Capel arrived, he and Bob developed a "wonderful" working relationship. *Courtesy University of Oklahoma Athletic Department.*

The OU basketball broadcast team prepares for a live broadcast from courtside. Left to right, producer-engineer Michael Dean, color analyst Mike Houck, and Bob.

It was a tumultuous 2006 season for the OU football squad. A week before fall practice began, Bob was shocked when he learned about returning quarterback Rhett Bomar receiving payment for work he was not doing at a Norman car dealership. Within days, Bomar and offensive lineman J.D. Quinn were kicked off the team. Paul Thompson, who had not practiced as the Sooner quarterback for a year, became the starter.

OU lost a highly controversial game against Oregon in which a local replay official blew the call on an onside kick which was the difference in the game. Following a loss to Texas, OU rebounded against Iowa State. However, on the last touchdown drive for the Sooners, star running back Adrian Peterson broke his collar bone when he was tripped up while sprinting into the end zone. Bob said, "It was a great disappointment for Peterson who had finished second in the Heisman voting the previous year as a freshman." [1]

OU nevertheless went on a seven-game winning streak, won the Big 12 South, and defeated Nebraska 21-7 to win the Big 12 title. In the Fiesta Bowl, OU lost to Boise State 43-42 in overtime because of the statue of liberty trick play that spawned a movie about the huge win for the Bronchos.

In Jeff Capel's first year as head basketball coach, the Sooners started strong but lost their final seven conference games in early 2007. OU missed any form of postseason play, snapping the nation's longest streak of 23 consecutive years.

The Sooner Football Network crew at the Tostito's Fiesta Bowl on January 1, 2007. Left to right, Bryan Stolte, Merv Johnson, Bob Barry, Mark Rodgers, Terry McLemore, Michael Dean, Tom Shores, Jim Wheeler, and Chris Stolte.

As for the football Sooners in 2007, OU opened the season with a 79-10 victory over North Texas, the most points scored by any team in the nation that day. In the next two weeks, OU beat the University of Miami 51-13 and Utah State 54-3. The Sooners beat Tulsa and then saw their national championship hopes take a huge blow when they lost to unranked Colorado 27-24 in Boulder after leading the Buffaloes 24-7 at halftime. OU beat Texas 28-21 and cruised through the Big 12 until losing quarterback Sam Bradford to a concussion and being upset by unranked Texas Tech. Even with the two conference losses, OU still made it to the Big 12 champi-onship game where the Sooners defeated Missouri, earning them a berth in the Fiesta Bowl. OU lost a BCS game for the second consecutive year to West Virginia 48-28.

From 2002 to 2007, OU produced three players that have had solid careers in the National Football League. *Courtesy University of Oklahoma Athletic Department.*

Blake Griffin was a superstar for OU. In 2009 he was named the nation's outstanding basketball player, the first Sooner to win that honor, and was the top pick in the National Basketball Association draft. *Courtesy University of Oklahoma Athletic Department.*

After signing McDonald's All-American Blake Griffin, Coach Capel's basketball Sooners showed incredible improvement in 2007 and finished 21-10 in the regular season. OU was seeded sixth in the NCAA Tournament where they defeated St. Joseph University in the first round before losing to number three seed Louisville in the second round. Sooner faithful were happy when Griffin announced at the end of the season he would return for his sophomore campaign at OU.

The KFOR-TV news team in 2006. Left to right, David Payne, Linda Cavanaugh, Kevin Ogle, Tammy Kaine, Kent Ogle, Sarah Stewart, and Bob.

When Bob celebrated a birthday at KFOR-TV, his fellow anchors presented him a birthday cake. Looking on are Kevin Ogle, left, and Linda Cavanaugh. As a surprise, Oklahoma City firemen appeared on the set to extinguish the fire expected from any lighting of the candles.

In 2008, Bob was named an Outstanding Alumnus of the Gaylord College of Journalism and Mass Communications at the University of Oklahoma. He was congratulated on the award by his sons, Bob, left, and Frank. *Courtesy University of Oklahoma.*

In 2008, Bob decided to officially retire from KFOR-TV which had been purchased the previous year by a private equity group, Oak Hill Capital Partners, and became part of Local TV LLC. Bob's fellow broadcasters and staff at Channel Four gave him a huge going-away party. It was appropriate for an unprecedented sports television career that spanned 43 years.

By 2008, the Sooner Sports Radio Network, with Bob, Merv Johnson, and sideline reporter Trent Smith, was heard on 38 radio stations in Oklahoma, New Mexico, Arkansas, Kansas, and Texas. KOKC Radio, formerly KOMA Radio, remained the flagship station of the radio network that was part of Sooner Sports Properties which controlled everything from radio broadcasts, to a 30-minute weekly video magazine with Coach Stoops, and even the signage in the stadium. The OU athletic department benefited greatly from the arrangement with Learfield Communications in a joint venture with Renda Broadcasting and Griffin Television.

On Tuesday nights during football season, Bob hosted "Sooner Sports Talk" with Coach Stoops from the Red Lobster restaurant in Norman. The network-wide show provided OU fans the opportunity to call and talk personally with the coach about OU football. On Thursday nights, Sooner assistant coaches appeared on a statewide call-in show on "Coaches Corner."

With Sam Bradford at quarterback, OU was ranked fourth in the 2008 pre-season Associated Press football poll. After scoring more than 50 points in back-to-back home wins over Chattanooga and Cincinnati, the Sooners jumped to number two in the poll. OU was ranked number one when Texas defeated the Sooners in the Cotton Bowl in Dallas 45-35. OU dropped to fourth.

Quarterback Sam Bradford won the Heisman Trophy in 2008. He was the fourth player to win college football's most coveted award while Bob was the radio voice of his team. *Courtesy University of Oklahoma Athletic Department.*

At the end of the regular season, Texas was upset by Texas Tech, throwing the Big 12 South into a three-way tie. Because OU was ranked higher in the BCS than the other two teams, the Sooners were tabbed to play in the Big 12 championship game, although Texas fans loudly cried foul. OU beat Missouri soundly in the title game and won the right to play for the BCS national championship at Dolphin Stadium in Miami. Unfortunately, the Sooners lost to Florida 24-14, three weeks after Bradford won the Heisman Trophy. It was the fourth time OU was playing for the national championship under Coach Stoops and the fourth Heisman Trophy winner for which Bob had broadcast every play of their collegiate career.

Not only did Bob have the privilege of broadcasting 2008 games for the Heisman Trophy winner, OU basketball experienced an incredible year in 2008-2009 when Blake Griffin was named as the player of the year in college basketball. Bob said, "It is a rare feat for any school to have a Heisman Trophy winner or the nation's top basketball player. To have both from the same school the same year is unbelievable, a tribute to the excellence of OU athletics." [2]

The OU basketball team started the 2008-2009 season 25-1, the best start in school history. Coach Capel's Sooners were granted a number two seed in the NCAA Tournament, beating Morgan State, Michigan, and Syracuse to advance to the Elite Eight. However, after hitting nine three-point shots during the previous game, Sooner guards were 0-for-15 for the first 35 minutes of the Elite Eight game against eventual national champion North Carolina, and lost to the Tar Heels 72-60. After the season, Griffin announced he would forego the final two years of collegiate eligibility and was selected by the Los Angeles Clippers as the first pick of the 2009 NBA draft.

After the NCAA Tournament, Bob underwent a left hip replacement surgery on April 28. Orthopedic surgeon Dr. Brock Schnebel, the OU team physician, had told Bob two years before that carrying extra pounds on his frame for 70-plus years had worn out his hips. Schnebel said, "When you overload the wagon, the wheels wear out." [3] Bob had both knees replaced eight years before.

Two months later, on June 10, Dr. Schnebel replaced Bob's other hip at the McBride Clinic Orthopedic Hospital. After Bob recovered, he could walk relatively normal for the first time in several years. The previous season he used a golf cart and wheelchair most of the time, especially getting to football stadiums or basketball arenas from parking areas.

OU's football opener on September 5, 2009, was a milestone in at least two ways. It was the first game to be played in Jerry Jones' new Dallas Cowboy Stadium in Arlington, Texas. It also was Bob's 650th college football broadcast, placing him at the top of a long line of distinguished radio broadcasters. For the 2009 season, KWTV sportscaster Toby Rowland became the sideline reporter for OU games. A graduate of Southern Nazarene University, Rowland had been covering OU sports for a decade. Eric Barnhart, general manager for Sooner Sports Properties, said, "Rowland is a good fit on the Sooner Network. He has already proven himself as a quality broadcaster." [4]

The 2009 Sooner football season was the "weirdest" Bob had ever seen. Quarterback Bradford injured his shoulder in the first half of the opening game against Brigham Young University. Bradford was basically lost for the season, although he tried to come back against Texas before reinjuring the shoulder minutes into the game. Bob said, "I have never even heard of a football team losing so many great players to injuries in a single season." In addition to losing the reigning Heisman Trophy winner, OU lost another first-round NFL draft prospect, tight end Jermaine Gresham, to injury in pre-season practice.[5] OU finished the disappointing season 8-5, although a "good" win over Stanford University in the Sun Bowl in El Paso, Texas, gave hope for the future.

Bob almost failed to make it to El Paso to broadcast the Sun Bowl game. When he carried his luggage from the Will Rogers World Airport parking garage to the terminal, he fell at the entrance to an escalator and took a huge spill, falling on his luggage. Fortunately, a hurt finger was the only casualty. When Bob and Toby Rowland boarded a Southwest Airlines flight to Dallas for a connecting flight to El Paso, the pilot announced the airplane could not take off because of a crack in the windshield. After more delays, Bob and Rowland arrived in El Paso 13 hours later.[6]

The 2009-2010 basketball season was also disappointing to Bob and Sooner fans. With several highly-rated young players, OU never played consistently and failed to make the NCAA Tournament.

Bob narrowly escaped injury in a February, 2010 game against Kansas at Allen Fieldhouse in Lawrence, Kansas. In the second quarter, OU player Tony Crocker was chasing a loose ball when he dived over the broadcast table and glanced off Bob's shoulder. As a shocked Bob was shown to the national ESPN audience, announcer Brent Musburger said, "There's Bob Barry, the king of radio sportscasters!"

A few minutes later, Bob received an e-mail from Big 12 Game of the Week announcer Dave Armstrong. The e-mail said, "Nice catch...of Crocker!"[7]

The close call with Crocker was reminiscent of an incident many years before at a basketball game at the field house at Texas

A & M. An Aggie player flew over the sideline table and "flattened" Bob and knocked his glasses from his head. The startled player, while lying on top of Bob, picked up the glasses and simply said, "Sir, here are your glasses!"[8]

At the end of the basketball season, Bob looked back on 50 years of broadcasting college football and basketball games. "I have enjoyed almost every minute of this incredible ride," he said. There was little question of how much he enjoyed life. Veteran sportscaster Ross Porter said, "Bob has one of the best laughs I have heard. He laughs frequently and makes everyone around him happier."[9] "Bob is funny," said Jane Jayroe. "That humor and his love of laughter is an enormous gift in a world so full of worry and pain. It doesn't mean he has been exempt from tough times, but he has found the sunshine and something to laugh about in most situations."[10]

May 5, 2010, was declared "Bob Barry, Sr. Day" in Oklahoma by Governor Brad Henry. Bob was overwhelmed by kindness shown by members of the state legislature as he addressed a joint session of legislators. At left is State Representative Weldon Watson who worked with Bob at Channel Four years before.

Bowl Championship Series (BCS) Executive Director Bill Hancock said:

Long ago, I found that even though Bob was my childhood hero, he was just one of us—a bright, kind-hearted, happy man with a gentle soul and a ready wit.

Bob is Everyman. And he treats every man and woman as if they are kings and queens. That is why we love him.[11]

Bob's sons have learned from watching their father. Frank said, "If there is anything Dad will leave behind for me and my children is the humbleness of doing your job to the best and yet just being a normal person and treating everybody else like they are normal."[12]

Bob Barry, Jr., believes his father is happiest with his cat, Fred, watching major league baseball in the privacy of his home where he has lived for more than 40 years in Norman. However, BBJ admits Bob is a master in a public setting, "He is so engaging and kind. He can walk into any room, strangers or friends, and just take it over. He is not fake. He is a great grandfather too!"[13]

Former OU basketball coach Billy Tubbs said, "It's not hard to be friends with Bob Barry. He's just so damn nice."[14] Bob admits that Tubbs was a "calming influence" when he made the transition from OSU to OU in 1991. OU football coach Bob Stoops said Bob's laugh is contagious, "When you are around him, you can't help but being glad you are alive and part of what is happening at the moment. He can bring happiness to any setting, any time. His ability to tell a joke during a busy football season helps keep things in perspective. No one is too busy for a joke."[15] Former OSU Coach Pat Jones said, "Bob always had a way of making us feel good on the job, on the golf course, or anyplace else where his big smile captured a room."[16]

In addition to being a nice guy, many applaud Bob's professionalism. Longtime WKY-Radio general manager and Bob's friend since high school, Dee Sadler, said, "Bob's love of sports and his infectious, enthusiastic personality make sports fun for the listener or viewer." [17] Oklahoma City insurance agent Richard Brown, who grew up in southeast Oklahoma listening to Bob's broadcasts of OU football and basketball games, said, "I like Bob's straightforward call of a game—he avoids the new-school slang expressions that most fans don't understand. I also like his honesty. If OU makes a mistake, Bob has no problem admitting it." [18] OSU football coach Mike Gundy says, "Bob has been a great friend to the OSU family. He somehow has been able to keep loads of friends at both state schools, no matter who he's calling games for." [19]

In the spring of 2010, Bob was preparing for yet another OU football season. He and his cat spend a lot of time together in their Norman home. "I eat a lot of TV dinners," Bob said. When he grows tired of frozen meat and vegetables he ventures to a nearby Norman restaurant, Sooner Dairy Lunch, where old friends serve him barbecue sandwiches and juicy hamburgers. He enjoys his role as a lay reader at St. John's Episcopal Church in Norman where he and several friends attend the 7:30 a.m. Sunday morning service and then eat breakfast together at a nearby Cracker Barrel restaurant.

Because of Bob's knee and hip replacements, he rides a motorized lift to his office on the second floor of his home. The office is adorned with dozens of photographs that cover his more than 50 years in broadcasting. It also contains stacks of media guides published by the athletic departments at OU and OSU. In a special place are his "spotter boards," the lifeline of his ability to tell listeners intricate details of the players, their hometowns, their physical description, and much more information. Visitors to the office can only imagine the thousands of hours Bob has spent preparing for upcoming game broadcasts.

It takes Bob eight hours to prepare a spotter board for a football game and three hours for a basketball game. He still uses push-pins like he did more than a half century ago when KNOR manager Bill Morgan asked him to be a play-by-play announcer. As Bob's OU football broadcast partner Merv Johnson said, "No one in the broadcast business works harder at preparing for a game. Bob is such a pro who labors over that spotter board like a set of twin babies." [20]

Bob Barry's life has been a dream—and the dream became real.

LEFT: Frank Barry and his children in 2010. Front row, left to right, Katie Barry and John Barry. Back row, Ellen Barry, Frank, and Amanda Barry.

BELOW: Bob Barry, Jr., and his family at Christmas, 2009. Front row, left to right, Evan Barry, Grace Barry, Gina Barry, and "BBJ." Back row, Mathew Barry and Tanner France.

NOTES

CHAPTER ONE

1   Interviews with Bob Barry, Sr., from February to September, 2009, Oklahoma Heritage Association Archives, Oklahoma City, Oklahoma, hereafter referred to as Bob Barry, Sr. interview.

2   Ibid.

3   Ibid.

4   Interview with Jack Glasgow Barry, December 30, 2009, Heritage Archives, hereafter referred to as Jack Barry interview.

5   Ibid.

6   *The Daily Oklahoman* (Oklahoma City, Oklahoma), June 8, 1938.

7   Bob Barry, Sr. interview.

CHAPTER TWO

1   Bob Burke, *The Oklahoma Health Center: A History* (Oklahoma City: Oklahoma Heritage Association, 2008), p. 31.

2   Bob Barry, Sr. interview.

3   www.en.wikipedia.org, "1931 in history."

4   *The Daily Oklahoman*, March 1, 1931.

5   www.en.wikipedia.org, "1931 in history."

6   Bob Burke and Von Russell Creel, *Lyle Boren: Rebel Congressman* (Oklahoma City: Oklahoma Heritage Association, 1991), p. 30

7   Ibid., p. 31.

8   Bob Burke and Gini Moore Campbell, *Lee Allan Smith: Oklahoma's Best Friend* (Oklahoma City: Oklahoma Heritage Association, 2005), p. 18.

9   Jack Barry interview.

10 Bob Barry, Sr. interview.

11 Jack Barry interview.

12 Ibid.

13 Ibid.

14 Roy P. Stewart and Pendleton Wood, *Born Grown* (Oklahoma City: Fidelity Bank, 1974), p. 59.

15 Bob Barry, Sr. interview.

16 Ibid.

17 Ibid.

18 Ibid.

19 Jack Barry interview.

20 Bob Barry, Sr. interview.

21 Ibid.

22 Jack Barry interview.

23 Bob Burke, Kenny A. Franks, and Royse Parr, *Glory Days of Summer: The History of Baseball in Oklahoma* (Oklahoma City: Oklahoma Heritage Association, 1999), p. 100.

24 Ibid.

25 Interview with Lee Allan Smith, December 7, 2009, Heritage Archives, hereafter referred to as Lee Allan Smith interview.

26 Ibid.

27 Bob Barry, Sr. interview.

28 *Glory Days of Summer*, p. 9.

29 bid.

30 *Oklahoma's Best Friend*, p. 31.

31 Bob Barry, Sr. interview.

32 Interview with Ralph Thompson, December 1, 2009, Heritage Archives, hereafter referred to as Ralph Thompson interview.

33 Bob Barry, Sr. interview.

34 Ibid.

35 Interview with Don Symcox, December 16, 2009, Heritage Archives, hereafter referred to as Don Symcox interview.

36 Ibid.

37 Bob Barry, Sr. interview.

38 Ibid.

CHAPTER THREE

1 Bob Barry, Sr. interview.

2 Letter from Ruth Hester to Bob Barry, May 14, 1952, Heritage Archives.

3 Bob Barry, Sr. interview.

4 Ibid.

5 Interview with Lee B. Thompson, Jr., December 4, 2009, Heritage Archives, hereafter referred to as Lee Thompson interview.

6 Ibid.

7 Bob Barry, Sr. interview.

8 Ibid.

9 Ibid.

10 Ibid.

11 Interview with Robert Bonnin Barry, December 10, 2009, Heritage Archives, hereafter referred to as Bob Barry, Jr. interview.

12 Bob Barry, Sr. interview.

13 Interview with Ross Porter, January 5, 2010, Heritage Archives, hereafter referred to as Ross Porter interview.

14 Ibid.

15 Don Symcox interview.

16 Henry Browne, Jr. and Bob Burke, *The Touchdown Club of Oklahoma* (Oklahoma City: Oklahoma Heritage Association, 2008), p. 44.

17 Ibid.

18 Ibid., p. 96.

19 J. Brent Clark, *Sooner Century: 100 Glorious Years of Oklahoma Football* (Coal Valley, Illinois: Quality Sports Publications, 1995), p. 54.

20 Jay Wilkinson, *Bud Wilkinson: An Intimate Portrait of an American Legend* (Champaign, Illinois: Sagamore Publishing, 1994), p. 95.

21 Ibid., p. 96.

22 Bob Barry, Sr. interview.

23 *Bud Wilkinson*, p. 97.

24 Bob Barry, Sr. interview.

25   *Bud Wilkinson*, p. 98.

26   *The Touchdown Club of Oklahoma*, p. 124.

27   Ibid., p. 125.

28   Lee Thompson interview.

29   Bob Barry, Sr. interview.

30   Ibid.

CHAPTER FOUR

1   www.americansportscastersonline.com, the official website of the American Sportscasters Association.

2   Ibid.

3   Ibid.

4   Jay. C. Upchurch, *Tales from the Sooner Sidelines* (Norman: Sports Publications, LLC, 2003), p.

5   Bob Barry, Sr. interview.

6   Ibid.

7   Ibid.

8   *The Daily Oklahoman*, September 14, 1960.

9   *Sports Illustrated*, September 9, 1968.

10   Robert Heard, *Oklahoma vs. Texas: When Football Becomes War* (Austin, Texas: Honeyhill Publishing, 1980), p. 266.

11   Bob Barry, Sr. interview.

12   *Bud Wilkinson*, p. 81.

13   Bob Barry, Sr. interview.

14   Ibid.

15   Ibid.

16   Ibid.

17   Ibid.

18   Ibid.

19   Lee Allan Smith interview.

20   *The Daily Oklahoman*, September 15, 1962.

21   *Oklahoma vs. Texas*, p. 279.

22   Bob Barry, Sr. interview.

23   Ibid.

24   Bob Barry, Sr. interview.

25   Bob Barry, Sr. interview.

26   Ibid.

27   *Tales from the Sooner Sidelines*, p. 65.

28   *Bud Wilkinson*, p. 85.

29   Bob Barry Sr. interview.

30   Ralph Thompson interview.

31   Bob Barry, Sr. interview.

32   *The Touchdown Club of Oklahoma*, p. 129.

33   Bob Barry, Sr. interview.

34   Ibid.

35   Ibid.

36   *The Touchdown Club of Oklahoma*, p. 131.

37   Bob Barry, Sr. interview.

38   *The Touchdown Club of Oklahoma*, p. 135.

39   Ibid.

40   Bob Barry, Sr. interview.

41   Ibid.

42   Bob Barry, Jr. interview.

CHAPTER FIVE

1   Bob Barry, Sr. interview.

2   *Oklahoma's Best Friend,* p. 102.

3   Ibid., p. 97.

4   Lee Allan Smith interview.

5   Interview with Jim Williams, February 10, 2010, Heritage Archives.

6   Ibid.

7   *Oklahoma vs. Texas*, p. 316.

8   Ibid., p. 323.

9   *The Daily Oklahoman*, October 12, 1966.

10   Bob Barry, Sr. interview.

11   Ibid.

12   Ibid.

13   Ibid.

14   Ibid.

15   *The Daily Oklahoman*, December 9, 1973.

16   Don Symcox interview.

17   Ibid.

18   Ibid.

19   *Oklahoma vs. Texas*, p. 329.

20   Bob Barry, Sr. interview.

21   *Oklahoma vs. Texas*, p. 335.

22   *The Daily Oklahoman*, April 3, 1967.

23   Bob Barry, Sr. interview.

24   Ibid.

25   *The Daily Oklahoman*, September 23, 1968.

26   *Oklahoma vs. Texas*, p. 347.

27   Ibid.

28   Bob Barry, Sr. interview.

29   Ibid.

30   Ibid.

31   *Oklahoma vs. Texas*, p. 369.

32   Bob Barry Sr. interview.

33   Ibid.

34   *Oklahoma vs. Texas*, p. 370.

35   Interview with Bob Dotson, January 15, 2010, Heritage Archives, hereafter referred to as Bob Dotson interview.

36   Bob Barry, Sr. interview.

37   Ibid.

38   Ibid.

39   Ibid.

40   Ibid.

41   *Oklahoma vs. Texas*, p. 382.

42   Ibid.

43   Ibid., p. 384.

44   Ibid., p. 385.

45   Ibid.

CHAPTER SIX

1   Interview with Larry Derryberry, February 3, 2010, Heritage Archives.

2   Bob Barry, Sr. interview, Lee Allan Smith interview, Lee Thompson, Jr. interview.

3   Bob Barry, Sr. interview.

4   Ibid.

5   Ibid.

6   Ibid.

7   Bob Dotson interview.

8   Bob Barry, Sr. interview.

9   Ibid.

10 "Requiem for a Bob Barry Fan," by Marguerite Quinn, Heritage Archives.

11 Ibid.

12 Bob Barry, Jr. interview.

13 Ibid.

14 Interview with John Franklin Barry, December 9, 2009, Heritage Archives, hereafter referred to as Frank Barry interview.

15 Ibid.

16 Ibid.

17 Bob Barry, Jr. interview.

18 Ibid.

19 Bob Barry, Sr. interview.

20 Ibid.

21 *The Daily Oklahoman*, April 9, 1997.

22 Bob Barry, Sr. interview.

23 Ibid.

24 Doris Dellinger, *A History of the Oklahoma State University Intercollegiate Athletics*, (Stillwater: Oklahoma State University, 1987), hereafter referred to as OSU Athletics, p. 285.

25 *Encyclopedia of Oklahoma History and Culture*, "Henry Payne Iba, "www.okstate.edu/encyclopedia.

26 *OSU Athletics*, p. 289.

27 Ibid., p. 290.

CHAPTER SEVEN

1 Lee Allan Smith interview.

2 Ibid.

3 Ibid.

4 Interview with Mick Cornett, January 27, 2010, Heritage Archives, hereafter referred to as Mick Cornett interview.

5 Bob Barry, Sr. interview.

6 *OSU Athletics*, p. 292.

7 Ibid.

8 Ibid., p. 298.

9 Interview with George Tomek, December 12, 2009, Heritage Archives, hereafter referred to as George Tomek interview.

10 Ibid.

11 Ibid.

12 Ibid.

13 Ibid.

14 Bob Barry, Sr. interview.

15 Ibid.

16 Ibid.

17 *The Daily Oklahoman*, August 28, 1977.

18 Bob Barry, Sr. interview.

19 *OSU Athletics*, p. 300-301.

20 Ibid.

21 *The Daily Oklahoman*, December 4, 1977.

22 Ibid., August 22, 1978.

23 *OSU Athletics*, p. 303.

24 Ibid., p. 307.

25 Ibid., p. 310.

26 Bob Barry, Sr. interview.

27 Ibid.

28 *OSU Athletics*, p. 310.

29 Ibid., p. 311.

30 *The Daily Oklahoman*, September 15, 1979.

31 Ibid.

32 Ibid.

33 Bob Barry, Sr. interview.

34 Pat Jones with Jimmie Tramel, T*ales from Oklahoma State Football*, (Champaign, Illinois: Sports Publishing LLC, 2007), hereafter referred to as *Tales from Oklahoma State Football*, p. 6.

35 *OSU Athletics*, p. 313.

36 Bob Barry, Sr. interview.

CHAPTER EIGHT

1 *The Daily Oklahoman*, September 8, 1980.

2 Ibid.

3 Ibid.

4 *Tales From Oklahoma State Football*, p. 22-23.

5 OSU Athletics, p. 330.

6 Interview with Jimmy Johnson, January 8, 2010, Heritage Archives, hereafter referred to as Jimmy Johnson interview.

7 Bob Barry, Sr. interview.

8 *Tales From Oklahoma State Football*, p. 34.

9 *OSU Athletics*, p. 343.

10 Bob Barry, Sr. interview.

11 *The Daily Oklahoman*, August 1, 1982.

12 Bob Barry, Jr. interview.

13 Ibid.

14 Ibid.

15 Ibid.

16 Ibid.

17 Bob Barry, Sr. interview.

18 *Tales From Oklahoma State Football*, p. 50.

19 Ibid., p. 52.

20 Ibid., p. 54.

21 Bob Barry, Sr. interview.

22 *Tales From Oklahoma State Football*, p. 66.

23 Ibid., p. 76.

24 2009 Oklahoma State University football media guide, Heritage Archives, *The Daily Oklahoman*, June 17, 1984.

25 Ibid., p. 83.

26 Bob Barry, Sr. interview.

27 *Tales from Oklahoma State Football*, p. 86.

28 Ibid., p. 90-91.

CHAPTER NINE

1 *Tales From Oklahoma State Football*, p. 102.

2 Bob Barry, Sr. interview.

3 Lee Allan Smith interview.

4 Bob Barry, Sr. interview.

5 *The Daily Oklahoman,* August 31, 1985.

6 Bob Barry, Sr. interview.

7 Ibid.

8 Ibid.

9 *Tales From Oklahoma State Football*, p. 106.

10 Mick Cornett interview.

11 *Tales From Oklahoma State Football,* p. 113.

12 Bob Barry, Sr. interview.

13 Interview with Linda Cavanaugh, January 21, 2010, Heritage Archives, hereafter referred to as Linda Cavanaugh interview.

14 Bob Barry, Jr. interview.

15 Linda Cavanaugh interview.

16 Ibid.

17 Ibid.

18 Ibid.

19 Ibid.

20 *The Daily Oklahoman*, November 16, 1986.

21 Ibid.

22 Interview with Jane Jayroe, January 31, 2009, Heritage Archives, hereafter referred to as Jane Jayroe interview.

23 Ibid.

CHAPTER TEN

1 *Tales From Oklahoma State Football*, p. 114-115.

2 Ibid., p. 115.

3 Interview with Mike Gundy, May 27, 2010, Heritage Archives, hereafter referred to as Mike Gundy interview.

4 Ibid., p. 119.

5 Ibid., p. 122.

6 Bob Barry, Sr. interview.

7 Interview with Pat Jones, February 3, 2010, Heritage Archives, hereafter referred to as Pat Jones interview.

8 *Tales From Oklahoma State Football*, p. 124-125.

9 Bob Barry, Sr. interview.

10 Ibid.

11 *Tales From Oklahoma State Football*, p. 138.

12 Bob Barry, Sr. interview.

13 *Tales From Oklahoma State Football*, p. 147.

14 Mick Cornett interview.

15 *Tales From Oklahoma State Football*, p. 148-149.

16 Barry Blog, by Robert Allen, October 15, 1988. www.okstate.com.

17 Ibid.

18 Bob Barry, Sr. interview.

19 Ibid.

20 Ibid.

21 Ibid.

22 *Tales From Oklahoma State Football*, p. 167.

23 Ibid., Mick Cornett interview.

24 *Tales From Oklahoma State Football*, p. 173.

25 Linda Cavanaugh interview.

26 Ibid., Bob Barry, Sr. interview.

27 *The Daily Oklahoman*, June 16, 1990.

28 Bob Barry, Sr. interview.

CHAPTER ELEVEN

1 Bob Barry, Sr. interview.

2 *The Daily Oklahoman*, November 16, 1990.

3 Ibid.

4 Bob Barry, Sr. interview.

5 Ibid.

6 Ibid.

7   *The Daily Oklahoman*, May 16, 1991.

8   Ibid., May 14, 1991.

9   Ibid.

10 Janis Teegins and Bob Burke, *He Got It!* (Oklahoma City: Oklahoma Heritage Association, 2003), p. 110.

11 Ibid.

12 *The Daily Oklahoman*, July 23, 1991.

13 Ibid.

14 Ibid.

15 Ibid., July 11, 1991.

16 Ibid., July 28, 1991.

17 Ibid.

18 Interview with Terry McLemore, May 13, 2010, Heritage Archives, hereafter referred to as Terry McLemore interview.

19 *The Daily Oklahoman*, October 2, 1991.

20 Ibid.

21 Ibid.

22 Ibid.

23 Interview with John Underwood, February 13, 2010, Heritage Archives.

24 Bob Barry, Sr. interview.

CHAPTER TWELVE

1   *The Daily Oklahoman*, October 16, 1992.

2   Ibid.

3   Ibid.

4   Bob Barry, Sr. interview.

5   *Tales from the Sooner Sidelines*, p. 165.

6   *The Daily Oklahoman*, September 15, 1992.

7   Bob Barry, Sr. interview.

8   *The Daily Oklahoman*, July 29, 1993.

9   *Tales from the Sooner Sidelines*, p. 173.

10 Interview with Kelvin Sampson, December 3, 2009, Heritage Archives, hereafter referred to as Kelvin Sampson interview.

11 Ibid.

12 Bob Barry, Sr. interview.

13 Interview with Bryan Stolte, March 17, 2010, Heritage Archives.

14 Ibid.

15 *Tales from the Sooner Sidelines*, p. 162.

16 Bob Barry, Sr. interview

17 *The Daily Oklahoman*, July 4, 1996.

18 Ibid.

19 Ibid., September 11, 1997.

29 Ibid., July 4, 1996.

21 *Tales from the Sooner Sidelines*, p. 170.

22 *The Daily Oklahoman*, April 5, 1998.

23 Bob Barry, Sr. interview.

24 *The Daily Oklahoman*, October 15, 1998.

25 Ibid.

26 Ibid., November 21, 1998.

CHAPTER THIRTEEN

1   Interview with David L. Boren, June 1, 2008, Heritage Archives, hereafter referred to as David Boren interview.

2   *Tales from the Sooner Sidelines*, p. 170.

3   Bob Barry, Sr. interview.

4   Ibid.

5   *The Daily Oklahoman*, March 14, 1999.

6   Ibid.

7   Ibid.

8   *Sooner Magazine*, Spring, 2003.

9   *The Daily Oklahoman*, June 3, 1999.

10 Ibid., June 30, 1999.

11 Ibid.

12 Ibid.

13 Bob Barry, Jr. interview.

14 Ibid., July 3, 1999.

15 *The Daily Oklahoman*, August 8, 1999.

16 Bob Barry, Sr. interview.

17 Ibid.

18 Letter from Bob Stoops to Bob Burke, March 1, 2010, Heritage Archives, hereafter referred to as Bob Stoops letter.

19 *The Daily Oklahoman*, December 31, 1999.

20 Kelvin Sampson interview.

CHAPTER FOURTEEN

1   Bob Barry, Sr. interview.

2   Ibid.

3   *The Daily Oklahoman*, November 1, 2000.

4   Bob Barry, Sr. interview.

5   Ibid.

6   *The Daily Oklahoman*, January 5, 2001.

7   Press release, University of Oklahoma Athletic Department, January 12, 2001, Heritage

    Archives.

8   Ibid.

9   Bob Barry, Sr. interview.

10 Ibid.

11 Ibid.

12 Ibid.

13 *Tales from the Sooner Sidelines*, p. 178-179.

14 Bob Barry, Sr. interview.

15 Kelvin Sampson interview.

16 Ibid.

17 Bob Barry, Sr. interview.

18 www.health.com/library/Alpha1

19 Bob Barry, Sr. interview.

20 Kelvin Sampson interview.

21 Ibid.

22 *The Daily Oklahoman*, July 29, 2004.

23 Bob Barry, Sr. interview.

24 Ibid.

25 *The Daily Oklahoman*, October 24, 2004.

26 Ibid.

27 Ibid., August 11, 2005.

28 Ibid.

29 Ibid., August 28, 2005.

30 Ibid.

31 Ibid., October 1, 2006.

CHAPTER FIFTEEN

1   Bob Barry, Sr. interview.

2   Ibid.

3   *The Daily Oklahoman*, June 11, 2009.

4   www.news9.com.

5   Bob Barry, Sr. interview.

6   Ibid.

7   Ibid.

8   Ibid.

9   Ross Porter interview.

10 Jane Jayroe interview.

11 E-mail from Bill Hancock to Michael Dean, December 21, 2009, Heritage Archives.

12 Frank Barry interview.

13 Bob Barry, Jr. interview.

14 Billy Tubbs interview.

15 Bob Stoops letter.

16 Pat Jones interview.

17 Dee Sadler interview.

18 Interview with Richard Brown, February 12, 2010, Heritage Archives.

19 Mike Gundy interview.

20 Interview with Merv Johnson, May 21, 2010, Heritage Archives.

INDEX

INDEX

INDEX